Kurt Tank
Ta 154

David Myhra

Schiffer Military History
Atglen, PA

Book Design by Ian Robertson.

We are interested in hearing from authors with book ideas on military topics.

Published by Schiffer Publishing Ltd.
4880 Lower Valley Road
Atglen, PA 19310 USA
Phone: (610) 593-1777
FAX: (610) 593-2002
E-mail: Schifferbk@aol.com.
Visit our web site at: www.schifferbooks.com
Please write for a free catalog.
This book may be purchased from the publisher.
Please include $3.95 postage.
Try your bookstore first.

In Europe, Schiffer books are distributed by:
Bushwood Books
6 Marksbury Avenue
Kew Gardens
Surrey TW9 4JF
England
Phone: 44 (0)181 392-8585
FAX: 44 (0)181 392-9876
E-mail: Bushwd@aol.com.

Try your bookstore first.

Kurt Tank Ta 154

About August/September 1942 the *Reichsluft-fahrtministerium (RLM)*, or German Ministry of Aviation, issued a surprising specification for a new flying machine. It was for a fast, twin-engined, multi-role night-fighting combat aircraft. This was unexpected, because the call for a night-fighter meant that the *RLM*, which was tightly controlled by *General Erhard Milch* and his head of aircraft planning, *Oberst Siegfried Knemeyer*, was finally admitting that they, too, were now thinking about defense of the *Reich*. This radical departure had its beginnings following heavy nightly offensive air raids by England's Royal Air Force (RAF). On the moonlit nights of 28/29 March 1942 the first German city went up in flames. This was Lübeck on the Baltic Coast, and a rather distant target for the RAF's first air raid on German soil. In all, 234 RAF aircraft, mainly *Wellingtons*, were dispatched, and using the *Gee* navigation aid dropped 144 tons of incendiaries and 160 tons of high explosives. At least half of the town was destroyed, mainly by fire, and 12 British heavy bombers never returned home, most of them being shot down along the route by German night fighters, a loss rate of 5 percent. Following the RAF's raid on Lübeck, *Adolf Hitler* demanded *Vergeltungsangriffe*, or reprisal raids, against England. Propaganda minister *Joseph Goebbels* said in a nationally broadcast radio speech:

"*Like the English we must attack centers of culture, especially those which have only little anti-defenses. Such centers must be attacked two or three times in succession and leveled to the ground...then the English will no longer find pleasure in trying to frighten us with terror attacks.*"

The *Ta 154* twin-engined two seat night-fighter as initially dreamed by *Kurt Tank*. About September 1942. Digital image by *Mario Merino*.

The RAF's next target was Rostock, also on the Baltic coast and the home factory of aircraft manufacturer *Ernst Heinkel, AG*. Between the two targets 780 acres of German urban area had burned...about the same number of acres which German twin engine bombers had destroyed during the Battle of Britain. RAF's Bomber Command felt the score was now about even, but then British bombers hit the heavily industrialized German city of Cologne, too, just for good measure. *Luftwaffe führer Hermann Göring* had acquired a new name, and much to his displeasure following these initial RAF air attacks in early 1942. Previously *Göring* had boasted about the "fortress" which Germany had become due to its military might. So certain was he and other *Nazi* leaders that no enemy air forces could ever penetrate the German *Reich* that if a single enemy bomb were ever to be dropped on German soil then the *Reich's* citizens should call him by the derogatory name of "*Myer.*" Yes, Germany had indeed built a military fortress...but after the RAF's first successful air attacks all the world knew that *Göring* had failed to put a roof over their fortress.

The *Luftwaffe* had night-fighters at the time Lübeck, Rostock, and Cologne were attacked. Under specifications given by *Hermann Göring*, the *Luftwaffe* had previously set up a *Nachtjagd* (night fighter group) and a chain of early warning radar (Radio Direction And Ranging) units, or boxes, on 17 July 1940. All

this was under the direction of *Oberst* (later *Generalmajor*) *Josef Kammhuber*. This so-called *Kammhuber Line* was somewhat similar to that which the British had built up around England. He had been instructed to develop a well-equipped night fighting force to protect German cities from the likes of RAF night-time bombers and quickly stop any possible further escalation. *Kammhuber* organized what he called the *Nacht- und Versuchsstaffel*. The *Luftwaffe* had had several small *Staffeln*, or squadrons, known as combined day and night fighting units. At first small and widely separated squadrons usually attached to a destroyer wing flew *Bf 109* fighters. After July 1940 they were combined into a single wing known as *Nachtjagdgeschwader NJG*, or night fighter wing. In addition to their earlier *Bf 109s* the *NJG* began receiving *Messerschmitt Bf 110C* twin engine *Zerstörer*, or destroyer, aircraft. The *Zerstörer* pilots did okay against the RAF but really needed specialized machines, not converted bombers, to be truly effective as increasing numbers of heavy bombers were sent into Germany. But a specialized night-fighter type had been strongly opposed by none other than the *Luftwaffe's* Quartermaster General, *Genealfeldmarschall Erhard Milch*. It was *Milch* who claimed that the small group of *Luftwaffe* night fighters could be adequately served by existing aircraft types such as the *Bf 110s* and *Ju 88s*. Thus, up until the RAF's raid on Lübeck, *Göring* and most of the others in the *RLM* were publically unwilling to think defensively, and any such talk was defeatist and could have very dangerous consequences for the speaker. Defense simply meant defeatist thinking, and it was completely contrary to the *Führer's* short-term military victory plans. This widespread thinking of offensive aircraft only in Germany changed forever in May/June 1942. That is when Bomber Command began their

1,000 bomber raids at night in a tightly-packed bomber stream all taking the same route against a single target. For example, Bomber Command put 1,046 bombers into the night air against the German city of Cologne on 30 May 1942. Only 898 bombers reached Cologne, the others missing their target completely, becoming lost, or turning back due to mechanical problems. The night attack lasted 90 minutes, during which 1,455 tons of bombs, mostly incendiaries, were dropped. This raid by the RAF of 1,046 bombers was twice as great as any the *Luftwaffe* had ever sent England during their losing Battle for Britain. Approximately 600 acres of Cologne, including about 300 acres right in the city's center, was totally destroyed. Forty-one RAF bombers representing 3.8 percent of the original force failed to return...about one half being shot down by German night fighters. Sixteen out of the 41 bombers shot down were claimed by *flak*

(*FliegerAbwehrKanonen*, or anti-aircraft guns) batteries. Another 116 returned in damaged condition, 33 suffered serious damage, while 12 bombers were considered damaged beyond repair. It was determined that the anti-aircraft (AA) or *flak* batteries in and around Cologne had succeeded in bringing down a poorly defended and protected RAF bomber every seven to eight minutes. This was not good enough to the German air defense planners, even though according to German reports, only 25 night fighters had been directed towards the RAF bombers as only 8 night fighter zones had been penetrated. They had done well, but really, Cologne's air attack defenses had been supersaturated and totally overwhelmed due to the bunching up of British night-flying bombers. This all new tactic on the part of Bomber Command was unpopular with their bomber crews because they preferred the old way of individually making their own way to the target.

A close-up view of the *Ta 154 V3* prototype with its *FuG 212* nose-mounted aerial array and fuselage cannon trough. This *Moskito* is seen from its nose starboard side. Digital image by *Mario Merino*.

get. But the bunching had resulted in only a 3.8 percent loss...much less than pilots that made their own way to the German targets. With the bunching of bombers all following the same route...the "bomber stream" practice of air attack had been born.

The bunching of enemy bombers at night now had to be quickly countered by the *RLM*. Initially, *Kammhuber* increased the coverage of his ground-based early warning radar and RAF night bomber losses started to rise again. What really made a difference was when *Kammhuber's* night-fighting *Ju 88s* and *Bf 110s* started getting an all new airborne radar system operating on 490 megacycle frequency. This airborne radar equipment was identifiable by those massive nose-mounted *FuG 202 Lichtenstein (Li)* aerial arrays known to the night fighter pilots as "barbed wire" and to the British as "mattress bedsprings." This initial *Telefunken* external radar aerial array would be

followed by improved smaller arrays such as the *FuG 212* and the *FuG 220*. Internal radar systems were being developed by the German electronics industry just prior to war's end. However, the search field covered by these nose-mounted antenna was 30% above and below and 60% to port and starboard. Thus enemy aircraft were picked up by the *FuG 202*, for example, at a distance corresponding to its own altitude. If the night fighter was cruising at 13,000 feet, the radio/radar operator could detect an enemy aircraft out to about 2 1/2 miles and as close as 600 feet.

In addition to *Lichtenstein*, the British bomber stream would be infiltrated with night-fighting *Bf 109s* and *Fw 190s* under a concept developed by a fanatical *Nazi* and a self-proclaimed "know it all" *Major Hajo Herrmann* which he called *Wilde Sau*, or "wild boar," an individual form of aerial hunting and killing. Although *Telefunken Lichtenstein's* maximum range of 2 1/2

miles and minimum range of 600 feet was very good for this initial German airborne radar, it had its shortcomings, too. First, it was unreliable. Secondly, the cathode-ray display was made up of three separate screens showing zig-zag lines: distance, vertical position, and horizontal (lateral) position. For the radio operator—now radar operator, too—came the new tasks of radio compass, fix bearings, communication with the ground staff and so on, all in all entailing an enormous amount of extra work. In addition, the flickering light blue cathode ray tubes dazzled the operator's eyes so much that after using the radar for 30 minutes he could no longer recognize the stars outside his cockpit canopy to identify if the zigs and zags were enemy bombers or fellow night fighters. Lastly, its seeming tangle of aerials and reflectors attached to the aircraft's fuselage nose acted as an air brake, impairing the night-fighter's handling characteristics and reducing, for example, a *Ju 88's* forward top speed by up to 15 mph. It was for these reasons that *Kammhuber* found that most of his pilots were initially unwilling to accept the unproven reliability of the radar and its performance-robbing *Lichtenstein* aerial array. But the airborne radar's unreliability was not due to the set itself but to its radar-assisted ground control system. It has been reported how night-fighter aces refused to have anything to do with the new *Lichtenstein* and other pilots followed their example. It was a common sight to see radar-equipped night-fighters parked near the hangars while those without the equipment were being flown. However, only one officer in *Kammhuber's* night-fighter group stuck with the *Lichtenstein* system, seeking to make it work. This was *Hauptmann Ludwig Becker*. He and his crew coaxed the electronic bugs out of their *FuG 202 Lichtenstein* to the point where they were making kills on very dark nights while their fellow non-radar

Moving around the machine we now view the *Moskito* from its nose starboard side out as it is parked out on the tarmac. Digital image by *Mario Merino*.

equipped night-fighters were not. As *Becker's* kill rate steadily increased other officers began following *Becker's* instructions on how to make the *202 Lichtenstein* work for them, too. So when the RAF had started its bomber offensive with the fire bombing of Lübeck and Rostock, *Kammhuber's* radar-equipped night-fighters were destroying on the average 3 out of every 100 bombers attacking Germany by night. On the other hand, *flak* 36 batteries destroyed about 1 out of every 100 night-flying bombers.

Although the *RLM* had several twin-engine fighters in March 1942, *Kammhuber* wanted a new machine to equip his four wings (*Geschwader*) of night-fighters. He had about 265 aircraft, of which 140 might be available on any given night. *Kammhuber* was accepting an expansion of new machines in March and April for his four *Geschwader*, and they included 33 *Bf 110s*, 20 *Ju 88s*, and 30 *Do 217s*. *Telefunken* had manufactured 275 *Lichtenstein* airborne radar sets, and production output was going on at the rate of 60 sets per month. As far as a new flying machine, *Kammhuber* had been talking with *Ernst Heinkel AG*, and they had pretty much independently designed a prototype night fighter, the *He 219*, which they claimed could be used as a specialized night fighter. This is where two strong men met eye-to-eye—*Kammhuber* and members of his night fighters wanted the *He 219* now because they felt it was that good. *General Erhard Milch* didn't like *Ernst Heinkel* much and didn't want his *He 219*. *Milch* and his planning department chief *Siegfried Knemeyer* told *Kammhuber* that he could have the specialized aircraft he and his crews wanted...that is, one designed from the ground up for night and bad weather fighting, but they would have to wait until one was designed and built. *Kammhuber* kept arguing that Germany couldn't risk waiting any longer, and besides, the night fighter he and his boys wanted had already been built by *Heinkel AG*. *Milch* and *Knemeyer* were not impressed.

A full starboard side view of the *Moskito* prototype.

The characteristics needed in a successful night fighter were pretty much apparent, *Kammhuber* argued. It had to be fairly large to carry the necessary weight of radar equipment, armament, and fuel. Also, two or even three men would be required to perform the specialized functions of flying, locating, and destroying an enemy aircraft in the dark of night. The night fighter must, however, be capable of a high rate of climb to reach the altitude of the bombers and do so very quickly. So any night fighting machine had to have a speed high enough to overtake any enemy bomber, relatively long range, and endurance to enable it to stay in the air and combat the stream of enemy bombers. The *He 219*, said *Kammhuber*, had all these qualities.

The ideal night fighter *Kammhuber* wanted Germany to design and build had to have other features, too. It must have a comparatively heavy armament, since the night fighter would usually get only one chance at their prey. If the first attack were not successful, the enemy bomber would disappear in the night. Since the trend in aerial combat was inevitably toward operations at ever higher altitudes, the night fighter had to be capable of good performance at high attitude and, finally, under the adverse conditions of darkness and often bad weather in which night fighting took place. Finally, it was desirable that a night fighter have good flying characteristics, particularly in landing and take-off.

Initially, *Messerschmitt's Bf 110* was pressed into night flying duties. It had been a failure as an escort fighter and long-range destroyer in the Battle for Britain, having needed itself to be protected by *Bf 109s*. But it did have some of the characteristics *Kammhuber* needed in a night fighter, and it was available, since it couldn't be used for the primary purpose for which it had been designed. The *Luftwaffe* also modified bombers, particularly the *Junkers Ju 88*, to serve as night fighters. Stripped down for night fighting, the *Ju 88* was relatively fast...faster than most British bombers...had a good rate of climb, and fairly good high-altitude performance. It was capable of carrying the necessary crew, armament, and fuel for a fairly long duration of flight. A number of specialized night fighters were proposed, and one, the *Heinkel He 219* "*Uhu*," or owl, was even produced in limited numbers. *General Kammhuber*, the chief of the night fighters, continuously demanded large-scale production of this machine; the few available were highly successful in combat, but it was never mass produced.

General *Milch* led the opposition to serial production of the *He 219*. He argued that although the performance of the "*Uhu*" was slightly superior to the modified *Ju 88*, the latter machine would be about as efficient in combat. In this argument *Milch* was supported by *Oberst Siegfried Knemeyer*, *Göring's* most trusted technical advisor. Even post war, *Oberst Knemeyer*, who came to the United States in "Operation Paperclip," maintained that the advantages of the *Heinkel 219* were not sufficient enough to warrant producing it as a night fighter as compared with the modified *Junkers 88*. According to *Knemeyer*, the *Ta 154* was a better machine for night fighting than was the *He 219*. *Knemeyer* stated that there were no revolutionary features in *Heinkel's 219* over *Junkers* and *Focke-Wulf*. Yet, when the *He 219* first appeared it was just in time to take advantage of a newly introduced and much more effective airborne radar system than those installed in earlier night fighters. This was an advantage. Yet *Heinkel's* machine had subtle advantages not readily apparent to members of the *RLM* but very important to the crews which flew it.

Heinkel's layout was such that visibility for the pilot was particularly good. Its handling characteristics, its crews reported, were outstanding. For example, failure of one of its two engines in flight did not lead to a critical situation as was common in other twin engine night fighters such as the *Ta 154*. Almost unique among *Luftwaffe* flying machines when the *He 219* was introduced was its tricycle landing gear. This feature made landings at night or under difficult conditions much easier and safer than aircraft types with the tailwheel arrangement.

Oberst Kammhuber argued that the *Heinkel He 219* had been tested in battle conditions, and its crews were calling the "*Uhu*" a successful machine for the purpose for which it had been designed. In its first experimental try-out on the night of 11-12 June 1943, a *He 219* flown by the night fighter ace, *Major Werner Streib*, destroyed five RAF "*Lancaster*" heavy bombers during a single flight. The "*Uhu*" was even reported as having shot down a *de Havilland* "*Mosquito*" bomber...the nemesis of the *Luftwaffe*. It was all in vain. *Kammhuber* persistently demanded large-scale

production of the *He 219*, but *Erhard Milch* and his technical office headed up by *Siegfried Knemeyer* persistently fought it, finally killing it on 25 May 1944 in favor of the proposed, untried *Ta 154* paper-only design by *Kurt Tank* of *Focke-Wulf*, as well as the other untried design by *Junkers*, their proposed *Ju 388J*.

Junkers' 388J was a modification of the standard *Ju 88* all-purpose machine, while the *He 219* would have given the *Luftwaffe* a very good night-fighter while the wood-built *Ta 154* was getting into production. Then again, the *Ta 154* had been designed specifically for night-fighting and might have been as effective as the *He 219*. In the end the *Luftwaffe* had no specially designed night-fighter. The *Ta 154* series production was canceled due to sabotage by concentration camp prison laborers and the destruction of the one-of-a-kind special glue factory by 8th Air Force *B-17* bombers. More about this later.

Even though *Milch* and *Knemeyer* killed the *He 219's* production on 25 May 1944, *Ernst Heinkel* tacitly ignored the order and limited production continued until the very end of the war. However, in the Fall of 1944, production of the *He 219* was again officially canceled by order of the *RLM*. It didn't matter, though, because the Red Army had overrun the factory producing the machine. About 300 of the aircraft had been produced, in contrast to the 2,000 *He 219's* *Kammhuber* had demanded. *Kammhuber* himself was fired as head of the night fighters in May 1943 when the RAF bombing attained the tempo and effectiveness that he had feared and predicted earlier. In a conference with *Hitler* at the time the irate *Führer* verbally attacked *Kammhuber*, his defeatism, his night fighter expansion plans, and his continuing opposition to *Milch* for canceling the *He 219*, yelling that *Kammhuber's* intelligence reports regarding the immense number of American bombers being produced

The *Ta 154 V3's* all wood vertical stabilizer/rudder appears bigger than life in this view. Digital image by *Mario Merino*.

each month were all lies...all Allied propaganda. *Kammhuber* foolishly begged to differ with the *Führer*, arguing that even his twin-engine night fighters were finding it difficult to cope with the widening range of British bombing of Germany on any given night attack. *Kammhuber*, too, believed that *Herrmann's* "*Wilde Sau*" activities would never stop the British Bomber Command, nor could the *Mosquito* be brought down by single engine fighters such as the *Bf 109* and/or *Fw 190* as *Herrmann* had been telling *Göring*. Now *Hitler*, as *Göring* had been told earlier, was being told by *Kammhuber* that the *Bf 110*, basically a heavy day-fighter, did not have the range to fly between areas of RAF bomber attacks. To get the range, *Kammhuber* stated, his men needed the new *Heinkel He 219*. In addition, the only way the RAF's Mosquito could be stopped was with the *He 219*. For all his comments he was fired where he stood...*Göring* sending him into exile in Norway. With *Kammhuber* gone he was replaced by *General Josef Schmid*. "Beppo" *Schmid* had commanded the *Hermann Göring* Division (Army) in North Africa. When the German Army surrendered there *Schmid* had been flown out, avoiding capture. *Schmid* was inexperienced in both flying and tactics, but he wore the "Blood Order of the (*Nazi*) Party" because in 1923 he had marched with them as a cadet. Among numerous changes made by *Schmid* was the wider use of *Major Herrmann's* "*Wilde Sau*," or freelance single-seater night fighters. They would range the length and breadth of Germany hunting down RAF bombers, landing only when they needed to refuel. Prior to this the "*Wilde Sau*" fighters operated within a few miles of their own airfields. Initially *Herrmann's* "*Wilde Sau*" was wildly successful. On the nights of 17 and 18

August 1943 Bomber Command attacked the *V-2* rocket establishment at Peenemünde in full moon light. After mistakenly scrambling over Berlin due to a diversion by RAF *Mosquitos*, the "*Wilde Sau*" night fighters finally regrouped over Peenemünde 100 miles away, catching the last wave of attackers, and shot down 41 of them...about 7% of the bombers. Six nights later Bomber Command attacked Berlin in the first of a series of heavy raids. On the night of 23 August Bomber Command put into the air 727 bombers, all headed for Berlin. Fifty-six RAF bombers failed to make it back to England...Bomber Command's biggest lost up until then. Then, on the night of 31 August 47 bombers didn't return from Berlin. On the night of 3 September, Bomber Command's final attack, 20 Lancaster bombers were shot down. The three raids on Berlin had cost RAF's Bomber Command 123 heavy bombers and crews, although causing considerable damage in the western sector of the city. As successful as "*Wilde Sau*" appeared to be at the time, *General Schmid* allowed German airborne radar to

fall into disuse, with the British continuing to improve technology even more. Later it would be painfully evident that with *Kammhuber's* firing, the suicide of *Generaloberst Jeschonnek* following a dispute with *Göring* regarding the RAF bomber attacks on Peenemünde and Berlin, and the disuse of airborne radar by his replacement *General Schmid*, the night-fighting *Geschwaders* never recovered from these three crushing blows. Germany had pretty much shot itself in the foot by ignoring the airborne radar guided night fighters when they concentrated on *Hermann's* "*Wilde Sau*." *Herrmann's* "*Wilde Sau*" would later come under fire, too, because it was argued that they only shot down RAF bombers while they were dropping their bombs over cities and German industry. "*Wilde Sau*" had no effect in stopping RAF bombers before they arrived over cities and industry. Later, *Herrmann* admitted that *Udet* had been correct in the numbers of bombers the *Allies* would put into the air over Germany and that Germany's fighter production, no matter how much production increased, would be overrated

As we walk around the *V3* the *Moskito's* port side wooden wing comes into view and is showing off its upper two tone camouflage. Digital image by *Mario Merino*.

whelmed by the Allies' steadily increasing number of bombers. *Herrmann*, too, came to admit that Germany would ultimately lose the war. In late Summer 1944 *Herrmann* was fired as *Kommandeur* of the 1ˢᵗ Fighter Division by *General* "Beppo" *Schmid* and sent into exile in Hungary. Recalled, he worked on a plan by which newly trained *Luftwaffe* pilots would ram their fighters into American *B-17* bombers. It is believed that as many as 20 *B-17s* may have crashed as a result of ramming. At war's end, on 9 May 1944, *Hajo Herrmann* was unwilling to surrender. Instead, he entertained ideas of joining the Red Army in the coming battle between America and the USSR. On 11 May he flew his *Fieseler* "Storch" to Budapest to see how he might be employed by the Soviets. It was not meant to be. *Herrmann* was placed in a Soviet prison where he remained until he was released on 12 October 1955 and returned to West Germany.

Returning to the *Ta 154*, after the three in a row incendiary bomb attacks on Lübeck, Rostock, and Cologne, the *RLM's Technische Amt* (Technical De-

partment) invited *Kurt Woldemar Tank* to prepare a study for a specialized two-seat night and bad weather fighter. *Kurt Tank* of *Focke- Wulf*, the father of the *Fw 190A*, had a great reputation in aviation circles. He was also the Vice President of the *Akademie der Luftfahrtforschung* (Academy of Aviation Research), and it was Tank whom leaders in the *RLM* turned to regarding the design for a night and bad-weather only fighter, and how the *Ta 154* came about.

Based on *Kurt Tank's* study for a specialized night and bad-weather fighter, the *Technische Amt* in September 1942 called for proposals for a twin engine fighter, but it was to be different from anything existing in the *Luftwaffe* aircraft stables. First, this machine was to be more powerful than existing so-called night fighters, that is, capable of two to three hours of flight duration and powered by the existing *Jumo 211*, but to be replaced with the more powerful *Jumo 213s* when they became available for field use. Secondly, this entirely new night-fighter was to be built as much as possible out of wood. Rapid development and quan-

tity production was highly emphasized, together with the extensive use of materials not in short supply...and that meant wood. So the *RLM* believed it could obtain a new night fighter design which used wood for the better part of its construction, thus, the German furniture industry could now become aircraft manufacturers. This, then, is how the *Ta 154* was born...a twin engine night-fighter of wooden construction and, to a large degree, inspired by the new British *de Havilland* "Mosquito," which had become a supremely successful application of wooden construction to a high-performance aircraft. Above all, this new German night fighter was to be ready for its maiden flight within twelve months, or about September 1943. Three aircraft companies were asked to submit their ideas for a new night fighter: *Heinkel AG*, *Focke-Wulf*, and *Junkers*. *Focke-Wulf's* response was their *Ta 211* and later changed to the *Ta 154* by the *RLM*. *Heinkel AG's* response was their *He 219*, and *Junkers* responded with their *Ju 388J*. Each of the three were considered very advanced designs at the time, while the *He 219* had already been tested in night-fighting operations and was found to be a good design for a night fighter. In November 1942, two months after the *Technische Amt* issued their September 1942 requests to industry, they chose the *Focke-Wulf* night-fighter entry.

Kurt Tank had designed three *Entwurfs* (drawings), each powered by *Junkers Jumo 211F* piston engines. *Entwurf 1* would be a single-seat *Schnellbomber* carrying a one-ton bomb load with a rear-firing cannon and a tail wheel. *Entwurf 2* was a design for a two man radar-equipped night fighter version with pilots seated in tandem and a tail wheel. *Entwurf 3*, also a radar equipped night fighter version, featured 2x*MG 151* 20 mm cannon in a *Schräge Musik* mounting in which the cannon were fixed in the fuselage and fired obliquely upward and forward (70%), a larger wing

Moving further around the *V3's* nose-mounted 4-pole *FuG 212* "mattress bedspring" radar array comes into good view. Digital image by *Mario Merino*.

area, and a nose wheel. The calculated maximum speed with a *GM-1* nitrous-oxide injection system, *Focke-Wulf* engineers claimed would be 451 mph [725 km/h] speed. This rate of performance was never reached.

A word about the *GM*-1 nitrous-oxide power boosting system is in order here. It was first referred to by the Germans by the code-name "*ha-ha*," nitrous oxide or "*laughing gas*" being injected into the engine's supercharger. The nitrous-oxide was retained under pressure in liquid form. The system was designated as *GM-1*. In a twin-engine machine such as the *Ta 154* the liquid was carried in three cylindrical containers arranged pyramid fashion, located in the fuselage aft of the radio/radar operator. Later aircraft had one 75 gallon cylindrical container. Compressed air cylinders contained the air used for forcing the liquid along the pipe lines into the engines. The complete installation weighed 400 pounds dry, and the weight of the nitrous-oxide was 900 pounds assuming full tanks. The tanks were heavily lagged with glass wool and enclosed in a shell of light alloy to prevent evaporation. In a *BMW 801* piston engine, for example, injection was arranged at two rates: normal flow at 7.95 pounds per engine per minute, and "emergency flow" at 13.2 pounds per engine per minute. The endurance of the *GM-1* injection boost system at the two rates was 45 minutes and 27 minutes respectively. This power-boosting system was used above the rated altitude of the engine. The nitrous-oxide provided additional oxygen for the engine, and also acted as an anti-deponent. Part of the increased power obtained was due to its charge-cooling qualities. With the *Jumo 213E* piston engine installed in some of the *Ta 154s*, when fed nitrous oxide at the "emergency flow" of 13.2 pounds per minute, for example, pilots increased their

horsepower from a take-off and/or emergency of 1,750 horses by 418 horses, or some twenty-five percent plus increase.

In addition to the *GM-1* power boosting system German aircraft engine makers had developed another system of injecting *methanol-water* 50%, more commonly known as *MW 50*. *MW 50* fluid consisted of 49.5 parts by volume of tap water, 0.5 parts of anti-corrosion fluid (*Schutzöl 39*), and 50 parts of methanol into *Daimler-Benz 603L* piston engines. An ethanol-water mixture could also be used in the *MW 50* installation on the *Junker Jumo 213A* piston engines. The mixture was carried in a cylindrical tank of 25 gallons per engine. Boost pressure from the supercharger was utilized to apply pressure to the tanks, forcing the mixture along a pipe to an injection nozzle in the eye of the supercharger. The *MW 50* system was used to obtain extra power below the rated altitude of the engine. The mixture was injected into the intake side of the supercharger and acted as an anti-detonate, providing charge cooling and enabling higher boost pressures to be used. It was expected that a 4% increase in power could be obtained even at constant boost pressure...the increased power being used for a maximum of 10 minutes at a time, and at least 5 minutes had to elapse between successive periods of

operation. At this increased power the spark plugs had a life of 15 to 30 hours.

Early in November 1942 *Focke-Wulf* received contracts to build 13 prototypes and 6 further airframes for stress (broken) and dynamic tests. Each of these initial prototypes were to be built at *Focke-Wulf's* facilities at Langenhagen near Hannover. *Kurt Tank* had hoped that both his single and two-seat fighter versions would be accepted for prototype construction, but the *RLM* was only interested in his nose wheel radar equipped two-seater version...*Entwurf 3*...for night and bad weather fighting. *Tank* abandoned his proposed *Entwurf 1* and *2* single and dual seat tail wheel versions.

Few people were surprised at the *RLM's* selection of *Focke-Wulf's Entwurf 3*...after all, *Kurt Tank* had pretty much justified the need for a specialized night and bad-weather fighter and went on to draw up the specifications for such a machine built of wood and what the German propaganda network of *Joseph Goebbels'* was calling the *Teutonic* "*Moskito*." *Focke-Wulf* had been previously allocated aircraft type numbers *152* through *154*. It is reported that *Tank* wished to keep the numbers *Fw 152* and *Fw 153* for two high-altitude *Fw 190* versions he was planning. He also did not want to use the assigned number "*211*" and

We see the *Ta 154 V3* parked out on the tarmac...however, appearing flight ready for a chance to go up and duel it out with RAF night bombers. Digital image by *Mario Merino*.

longer, either, and in fact the *RLM* later gave it to *Hütter* for their series work on a derivative of the *He 219*. Thus, *Tank* got his way and the *RLM* created a new designation of *Ta* for *Tank* and designated his new night and bad-weather fighter from *Focke-Wulf* as the *Ta 154 Moskito*.

Since the *RLM's* request called for a rapid quantity production machine with a view to conserving steel and light alloys, *Tank* chose a primarily wooden structure for his *Ta 154* proposal...just as he had suggested in his earlier written report to the *Technische Amt. Kurt Tank* commented post war that when he was writing his report on the need for a specialized night and bad-weather fighter, he had copied the *de Havilland "Mosquito."* It, too, was built largely out of wood. In reality the composition of *Tank's Ta 154* was 57% wood, 30% steel, 13% various material, and almost no aluminum. Like the *de Havilland*, *Tank* nicknamed his night fighter the *Deutsches "Moskito,"* showing that imitation is perhaps the sincerest form of flattery. Although the *Ta 154* was often claimed by German radio to be the counterpart of *de Havilland's "Mosquito,"* its only similarity

was in the materials used in its construction. *Tank* said post war that the shortage of steel and aluminum alloys had forced Germany back upon wood, which he said was the classical material for aircraft construction. New laminating processes had been perfected, he said, for making it more reliable in use and for the construction of thin walls of fighter airplanes. In the case of the *Ta 154 Moskito*, German furniture makers could be ordered to help those airplane builders who now wanted to construct fighter aircraft out of wood. Surprising, too, although *Tank* won the competition due to the widespread use of wood, he had said privately to *Göring* that he didn't favor wooden wings because wood did not lend itself to a smooth enough finish, which, by the way, would have come as quite a surprise to the *Horten* brothers whose smooth wooden outer wings on their all-wing *Ho 9 V1* appeared as glass. Then again, *Tank* told *Göring* that "a single fly which left its droppings on the wing's forward leading edge was enough to undo the whole laminar effect." In fact, *Kurt Tank* really preferred metal to wood. At *Focke-Wulf* design of the wooden *Ta 154* would be

under the guidance of *Oberingenieur Ernst Nipp* and his team, which were located at the company's *Entwurfsbüro* (design office) in Bad Eilson. Then when the *211/154's* proposal was accepted by the *RLM*, it was turned over to the company's *Konstruktionsbüuro* (design office), also at Bad Eilson. In addition to *Ernst Nipp* were senior engineer *Ludwig Mittelhuber*, chief aerodynamicist *Gotthold Matthias*, and engineer *Herbert Wolff*. The first prototype, the *Ta 154 V1*, was completed within ten months of *Focke-Wulf* receiving the *RLM* contract. Several weeks into flight testing the *RLM* gave *Focke-Wulf* an order for 250 *Ta 154A-1* night fighters. The *Reichkriegministerium's* Otto Saur (an official in *Albert Speer's* war-time emergency planning organization established to boost fighter aircraft production) was so taken with the possibilities of the wooden *Ta 154* he believed that when manufacturing facilities were fully established by the end of 1943, an output of 250 *Ta 154s* per month might be possible. *Saur's* plan called for two manufacturing facilities in Poland where 80% of the 250 *Ta 154s* per month would be produced: Kreising and Messengelände near the city of Posen (now known as Poznan). Several other manufacturing sites included Erfurt in Germany and Breslau (now known as Wroclaw) in Poland.

In the mid 1980s this author interviewed *Gotthold Matthias* in his Redondo Beach, California, home. *Matthias* said that it wasn't *Ernst Nipps'* intention to copy the *de Havilland "Mosquito"* then flying, but as their *Ta 211* progressed through its design stages it just seemed to turn out looking like the British twin-engine fighter. The *Ta 211*, too, came to have a shoulder-level one piece wing...like the *"Mosquito,"* and so on. British aviation designers, post war, said that *Tank's* final *Ta 154* wasn't as graceful in appearance as their *Mosquito* from the Hatfield, Hertfordshire, workshop. They said *Tank's* design elements gave it a clumsy

It appears that RAF night bombers have been sighted and the *V3* has been ordered to intercept. Digital image by *Mario Merino*.

look. Furthermore, the British pointed out, the *Ta 154's* wing's were too small, its twin *Jumo 213A* piston engines appeared too large in diameter, and the 3-bladed *Junkers VS-11* variable-pitch wooden propellers were too fat. In addition, they added, the large radar installation gave the *154* a balky, ugly look to its nose. Wow! With *Jumo 213A* piston engines the *Ta 154* was capable of 392 mph [630 km/h] at an altitude of 27,887 feet [8,500 meters]. On the other hand, the *de Havilland* "Mosquito" from Hatfield with its twin *Rolls-Royce* "Merlin 21" piston engines could reach 385 mph [620 km/h] speed at 20,669 feet [6,300 meters] altitude. The *Ta 154*, it appears, could only safely attack *de Havilland* "*Mosquitos*" at relatively safe altitudes...not much of an advantage, it was later learned, and even much less so when a fully armed *Ta 154* with its two man crew was not sufficient to destroy the highly respected *de Havilland* "Mosquitos" during their night attacks within the *Third Reich.*

The first prototype *154V1* (*werk nummer 100001 TE+FE*) was powered by two 1,350 horsepower (for take off) *Junkers Jumo 211R* 12-cylinder liquid cooled engines with annular radiators, driving broad-blade propellers. The *Jumo 211R* was rated at 1,480 horsepower for cruising at 9,850 feet altitude, while older versions of the *211* were currently powering the *Heinkel He 111* medium bomber. The *154 V1* was flown on its maiden flight by *Focke-Wulf's* chief test pilot *Hans Sander*, along with flight test engineer *Walter Schorn* at Langenhagen (near Hannover) on 1 July 1943. The test flight lasted about one hour. A nearly identical *Ta 154*, the *V2* (*werk nummer 100002 TE+FG*), was completed several days later. It differed only from the *V1* in that it had 2x*MK 103* 30 mm cannon and 2x*MG 151* 20 mm cannon installed. Both machines were extensively tested by *Luftwaffe*-based Rechlin aircraft test pilots. The *154 V1* and *V2* were

The *V3* is gaining altitude as it leaves its airfield behind. Its pilot still has to pull in its tricycle landing gear. Digital image by *Mario Merino*.

also flight tested in comparison to the *Heinkel He 219.* During these tests Rechlin test pilots claimed a level speed of 435 mph [700 km/h] at an altitude of 19,685 feet [6,000 meters] altitude, but this was without the usual equipment, radar, or heavy armament.

The *Focke-Wulf* engineers' engine of choice was the *Junkers Jumo 213E* with their three-speed, two-stage superchargers and rated at 1,750 horsepower for take-off and 1,330 horsepower at 32,810 feet altitude. But since it was not yet available the first *154 Moskito* prototypes (*V1* and *V2*) were powered by *Jumo 211Rs*. The next part of the flight tests at Rechlin were cannon firing tests. For this test only the *V2* was used, and these tests did not go as well as had been hoped. For example, it was found that the wooden forward section of the *V2's* fuselage could not withstand for long the shocks and vibration that accompanied the firing of its four cannon, and extensive reinforcement of this portion of the fuselage was found to be necessary. Later an improved stiffer forward fuselage and cockpit area was constructed, and it was first

tested by towing it under water to actually test it for stiffness. These so-called "barge tests" were done in the Spring of 1943 at Lake Alatsee, near the village of Füssen in Bavaria, by the *Luftfahrt Forschungsanstalt Graf Zeppelin* (*FGZ*), or aircraft research establishment. It was known that the dynamic pressure acting on a body moving at high velocity through air could be simulated with considerable accuracy at much lower speeds in the denser medium of water. *Kurt Tank* said post war that the forward fuselage of a *Ta 154* was hung beneath a floating rig fitted with measuring instruments and hauled through the water at progressively higher speeds by power-driven cable winches.

The *Ta 154 V1* was first flown on 1 July 1943 at Langenhagen by the *Mustereprobung* (prototype test center) headed by *Dipl.-Ing. Hans Sander* with fitted with twin *Jumo 211F* piston engines. This was *werk nummer 100001* and was given the radio call letters *TE+FE*. The machine achieved only 389 mph [626 km/h] speed in level flying with *Focke-Wulf* company test pilot *Hans Sander* in the cockpit. *Kurt Tank* flew

this machine on 7 July 1943, and hydraulic problems forced a premature landing to the planned flight test. Next came the *154V1A*, which was an *Attrappe*, or mockup. The similar *V2 werk nummer 100002 TE+FF* was completed next, and it had the *FuG 212 C-1 Lichtenstein* radar. The *V2* was also used to obtain additional static vibration data. These and the following development aircraft were built using the *Tego-Film* special adhesive-glue developed by the *Goldmann Werk* in the city of Wuppertal.

On 25 November 1943 the third prototype *Ta 154V3 (werk nummer 100003 TE+FG)* was flown on its maiden flight to the *Führer-Hauptquartier* at Insterburg (now known as Chernyakhovsk, Russia). Flying along side on the 500 mile [805 kilometer] trip was the *Ta 154 V1*. Waiting at Insterburg were *Hitler* and other high *Third Reich* officials who had gathered

there for a demonstration of modern weapons. The *V3* was intended to serve as a prototype for the pre-production *Ta 154A-03/U1* machines. The *V3* carried a *FuG 212 Lichtenstein C1* radar array and was powered by two *Junkers Jumo 213E* engines providing 1,750 horsepower for take-off and 1,580 horsepower for climb and combat at sea level. The *Ta 154V3* was the first machine to carry full armament, suffering a 12 percent loss in maximum speed (47 mph [75 km/h]) as a result of the drag from its cannon, the *Matratzen* nose-mounted radar aerials, and necessary exhaust flame dampers. It apparently didn't matter to the *RLM*, because they placed an order for 250 of them and designated it the *Ta 154A-1*.

Additional *Versuchs* (research) prototypes were completed during the early months of 1944 and tested with various types of radar equipment and arrays.

These machines included the *Ta 154V4 (werk nummer 100004 TE+FH)*, which flew on 19 January 1944, and *Ta 154V5 (werk nummer 100005 TE+FI)*, which flew on 23 February 1944. One of the seven prototypes crashed when an engine overheated during single-engine flight testing. The *FuG 212* radar array was later replaced by a single centrally-mounted pole on some pre-production examples, while others continued to carry the *Hirschgeweih* (Stag's Antlers) array for the *FuG 220 Liechtenstein SN-2*, and a housing above the cockpit for the rotating aerial of a *FuG 350 Naxos ZH2S*...RAF radar emission receiver. Other equipment included a *Revi 16B* gun sight, a *FuG 10P* H.F. communications set, *FuG 16ZY* V.H.F. radio, *FuG 25a* I.F.F., *FuG 101a* radio altimeter, a *FuB1 2* blind approach receiver, and a *PeGe6* radio compass.

The *RLM* forced into service many wood-working shops as sub-contractors to *Focke-Wulf*. Eight *Ta 154A*-0 pre-production machines were completed at the Erfurt factory during June, July, and August, with the first production *Ta 154A-1* flying on 13 June 1944. These machines were delivered to a service test center for flight testing, but were withdrawn after only several days in order to carry out experimental work...six of the *154A-0*'s being modified for the "*Mistel*" role. Warheads were fitted in their forward fuselages and superstructures attached to carry *Fw 190* "*director fighter*." At the same time work was continuing on the second order of series production *154A-1s* being built at Erfurt, as well as at Posen, Poland.

A second series production *Ta 154A-1* crashed at Erfurt on 28 June 1944, coming apart during a high-speed test run. According to *Gotthold Matthias*, it was later determined that the adhesive used to glue wood pieces contained acid, which in turn weakened the joints. "*Kurt Tank* immediately halted the series production line while investigations were carried out. We discovered," said *Matthias*, "that the prison labor force

The *V3* climbs to meet and do damage to the bombers. Digital image by *Mario Merino*.

was pouring their collective urine into the glue pots...hence the *source* of the glue-weakening acid." About the same time, the first series production *Ta 154A-1* from the Posen factory crashed on 18 April 1944 during a landing approach. "This time the cause was not blamed on faulty glue, but instead was due to the failure of a landing flap during a landing approach," said *Matthias*.

On 18 June 1943 the *RLM* ordered 250 *Ta 154* built in series as night fighters. Series production was set up in three locations: Posen, Breslau, and Erfurt. Posen-Kreising was where a brand new *Focke-Wulf* assembly plant was located with its own airfield and finished in August 1943 by an estimated 2,000 Jewish workers. Upon completion this entire labor force was sent to Auschwitz *KZ* in September 1943. It is believed that only seven *Ta 154A-1s* were completed at Posen, and all of the fully assembled *Ta 154A-1s* were delivered to a service unit. One interesting feature of the *Ta 154A* was its landing gear, with the so-called "levered-suspension main shock-absorber units," and the extremely shallow front fuselage with the cockpit fairing flush with the upper surface of the wings. *Tank* claimed that the practical development of the nose-wheel landing gear made for greater safety on returning from a sortie in the event of a forced landing. The nose wheel, when retracted, lay flat under the forward part of the cockpit.

Posen-Kreising also completed six examples of the *Ta 154* "*Sprengstoffträger*," which were intended as bomber destroyers, a warhead being installed in their fuselage nose by moving the cockpit further aft and a downward-firing ejector seat being fitted for the pilot. It was proposed that the *Ta 154* pilot should aim his aircraft at the enemy bomber and then eject himself downward from the cockpit just before contact was made. However, none of these *Ta 154* bomber destroyers were ever flown, and it appears that no attempt was made to re-instate the *Ta 154 Moskito* in Germany's aircraft production program.

The Breslau assembly facility was the former *Famo Fahrzeug und Motrenwerke GmbH* while the assembly plant at Erfurt was known as the *Reparaturwerke*-Erfurt (*RLM Werke Nummer 068*). The *RLM* expected deliveries to start in January 1944 with completion of the 250 work order to be completed by November 1944. It was anticipated by *Otto Saur* that by Summer 1945, monthly deliveries of the *Ta 154* from all sources would reach 250 machines. The *Ta 154 V3* was first flown on 24 November 1943 for 15 minutes and then demonstrated to *Hilter* and other high officials. This machine was powered by twin *Jumo 211F* (later *211N*) engines with an armament of 4x*MG 151* 20 mm cannon.

Late in 1943 the three production centers were reinforced with labor to go into mass production. To Posen the *Focke-Wulf*-Cottbus plant was added to build pressurized cockpit cabins and fuselages. *Famo* opened a new facility in Bunzlau, where 1,500 prisoners of the *Gross-Posen KZ* labored to build components for the *Ta 154*. Erfurt acquired the *Holzflugzeugbau-Gotha* (*RLM Werk Nummer 091*), which was located about 15 miles [24 kilometers] from Erfurt.

The 25 prototypes built at Langenhagen had nothing to do with the series production. But on 5 August 1944 six or seven of the 25 prototypes were destroyed

A view of the *V3* from its port side with its *FuG 212* airborne radar array looking like the nose of a giant insect. This machine's engine exhaust flames are being suppressed so that the RAF cannot identify the *Moskito* as it hunts for the trespassing bomber in the darkness. Digital image by *Mario Merino*.

on the ground from a bombing raid by American 8th Air Force B-17s. Lost were the Ta 154 V1a, V2, and V3 prototypes. In addition, the V7 suffered approximately 70% damage, the V15 30% damage, and the V22 60% damage.

On 1 March 1944 the Jägerstab of Otto Saur laid down the following short-term delivery schedules for the Ta 154 mass production: Posen-Kreising was to deliver 37 machines by May 1944, Erfurt 21 machines, and Breslau 5 machines. Unfortunately, the American 8th Air Force bombing started soon after. On 9 April 1944 Posen was attacked by 33 B-17s and again on 29 May. It is for this reason the first Posen-built machines, the A-1 werk nummer 320003 KU+SP, made its maiden flight only on 18 April 1944 and crashed on its landing approach. Its test pilot Werner Bartsch survived, although he spent seven months in a hospital. Another seven machines were flown by 14 August, and at this date werk nummer 320059 was also finished. Thus, Posen built with the help of Cottbus 57 A-1s, A-2s, and A-4s. Cottbus itself was attacked by USAAF 8th bomb squadron B-17 and B-24 bombers on 11 April, and again along with Sorau and Posen on 29 May 1944 dropping incendiary bombs. Posen was hit by no fewer than 58 B-17s. This raid on Posen halted production of Ta 154s there for over three months.

The Erfurt production also had been attacked by American bombers on 20 July 1944. But it was still able to assemble 64 machines along with the help of Holzflugbau-Gotha. The last Ta 154 assembled at Erfurt was werk nummer 120064. Only a few of the 64 Ta 154s were flown. Famo was only able to deliver five Ta 154s by May 1944 with 2,500 male KZ labor coming from Bunzlau. It is believed that Kurt Tank himself stopped production of his Ta 154 given the loss of the Goldmann Werke wood glue and possible sabotage by KZ workers during assembly of component parts. Nevertheless, the RLM withdrew its initial order for series production and redeployed the underground aircraft production facility at Salzbergwerk-Bremen.

The Ta 154 had a high priority status (Class 1 night-fighter), Otto Saur's Jägerstab mobilizing new facilities for its mass production. The underground Focke-Wulf factory and Salzbergwerk-Bremen was used for assembly of Ta 154 fuselages. The Flugzeugwerk Mielec (FWM) in Poland had first opened in October 1938 building the P.37 bombers with a planned production of 450 bombers annually. After the war started, 5,000 men worked under Heinkel AG supervision to build the He 111 and the He 177. From 9 March 1942 labor for FWM was provided by 2,000 Jewish laborers from a KZ built nearby by SS Führer Himmler. FWM was attacked by the USAAF on 25 July 1944 by 33 P.38s. In addition the production line was notorious for sabotage actions by the prison-camp workers. Finally, early in August 1944 due to the advancing Red Army FWM was closed. It had only produced 14 Ta 154 fuselages and wings.

Otto Saur's Jägerstab Flugzeug Programm of 3 June 1944 still called for the series production of four Ta 154 subtypes: A-1 and A-3 two-seat day fighters; the A-2 single-seat day fighter; the A-4 two-seat night fighter; and the C-2 destroyer version. These subtypes include:

Kurt Tank's two-seat night fighter Ta 154 V3 shown from its port side sporting its nose-mounted FuG 212 radar Matratze (mattress bedspring) aerial array and fuselage-mounted cannon. In late 1942, the FuG 212 had superceded the 202 and 200, which were the first German airborne designed radars and built by the giant Telefunken Electronics Werke. Digital image by Mario Merino.

• **Ta 154A-0** - two seat night fighter prototype powered by twin *Jumo 211F* piston engines turning *VS-11* 3-bladed wooden propellers and equipped with *FuG 212* radar. It is believed that eight *Ta 154A-0s* and fourteen *Ta 154A-0/U1s* were completed.

• **Ta 154A-1** - two seat day fighter powered by twin *Jumo 211F* piston engines turning *VS-11* 3-bladed wooden propellers and featuring 2x*MG 151* 20 mm plus 2x*MK 108* 30 mm cannon.

• **Ta 154A-2** - single seat day fighter (the prototype was the *V15*) powered by twin *Jumo 211N* piston engines turning *VS-9* 3-bladed wooden propellers and featuring a 66 gallon [300 liter] fuel drop tank.

• **Ta 154A-3** - two seat trainer type based on the *Ta 154A-1* series featuring the *VS-9* 3-bladed wooden propeller. Approximately 20 machines were to be assembled, however, none were.

• **Ta 154A-4** - two seat night fighter series of limited production powered by twin *Jumo 211N* piston engines and featuring a *FuG 212A* and *FuG 220* radar. Maximum speed approximately 395 mph [635 km/h].

It appears that several additional advanced so-called *Ta 154B* production versions were planned and include:

• **Ta 154B-1** - a two-seat night fighter with an all metal nose section and powered by twin *Jumo 211N* piston engines and similar to the *Ta 154A-4*. This version was canceled sometime in 1943.

• **Ta 154B-2** - a single-seat day fighter with an all metal nose section, powered by twin *Jumo 211N* piston engines and similar to the *Ta 154A-2*. This version was also canceled sometime in 1943.

The outstanding differences between the *A* and *C* sub-types of the *Ta 154* were, in the latter, the installation of two *Junkers Jumo 213A* piston engines, a metal nose and, in the night fighter version, 2x*MK 108* cannon in the rear of the fuselage firing forwards and obliquely (*Schräge Musik*) upwards at an angle of approximately 70% from the horizontal. In the day fighter versions the upward-firing cannon were omitted, but mountings were provided in the sides of the fuselage for 2x*MK 108* cannon as an alternative installation to the 2x*MK 103* and 2x*MK 151* cannon. A noticeable fuselage modification was the introduction of a "bubble" type cockpit canopy, thus altering the otherwise flat top to the fuselage of the *Ta 154A*. The *Ta 154C-1* night fighter also had a pilot-ejection seat. Two wing fuel tanks, each with a capacity of 48 gallons, were to be fitted to the *Ta 154C-1*. Performance of the *Ta 154C-3* version was a maximum speed (with *GM-1*) of 428 mph [685 km/h] at 32,800 feet [10,000 meters] attitude. These *C* sub-type versions include:

• **Ta 154C-1** - two seat night fighter featuring a redesigned metal nose section with a raised cockpit, hinged cockpit canopy, ejection seats, extended rear fuselage and powered by twin *Jumo 213A* piston engines. It is believed that between six to ten prototypes were to have constructed and included the: *V8*, *V10*, *V16*, *V17*, *V18*, *V19*, *V20*, *V21*, *V22*, and *V23*. It is thought, too, that up to 1,800 *Ta 154C-1s* were to have been constructed by October 1945 by production facilities located in Erfurt and Posen.

• **Ta 154C-2** - a single seat day fighter/bomber featuring a sliding cockpit canopy, *GM-1* injection sys-

A beautiful nose port side view of the *Moskito* chasing down a RAF night bomber over Germany. Digital image by *Mario Merino*.

tem, and capable of carrying one or more *SC* bombs of unknown poundage (kilogram weight). This version, of which *V21* was to be its prototype, was canceled about May 1944.

• *Ta 154C-3* - two seat day fighter with all the features of the *C-1* in addition to split landing flaps. Initially conceived as a photo reconnaissance aircraft.

• *Ta 154C-4* - two seat day fighter/bomber with all the features of the *C-1*. Proposed and canceled about June 1943.

Two high altitude *Ta 154D* sub-types were planned and included:

• *Ta 154D-1* - high attitude two seat night fighter powered by twin *Jumo 213E* piston engines. Redesignated as the *Ta 254A-1*.

• *Ta 154D-2* - high altitude single seat destroyer powered by twin *Jumo 213E* piston engines. Redesignated as the *Ta 254A-3*.

One interesting planned version of the *Ta 154* was known as the *Ta 254*, a projected high altitude, longer wing-span development of the *154D* with a wing area of 453 square feet [42 square meters] and an all-up weight of 25,300 pounds [11,490 kilograms]. Both day and night fighter versions were anticipated. Armament for the *Ta 254* night fighter was to be 2x20 mm *MG 151* and 2x30 mm *MK 108* cannon or 6x30mm *MK 108* cannon, all firing forward, and 2x*MK 108* cannon in the fuselage rear and firing obliquely upwards. The day fighter was to have a fixed forward-firing armament of 2x*MG 151* (200 rounds per cannon) and 2x*MK 103* (100 rounds per cannon), with the possible alternative of 6x*MK 108* cannon. Power plant for the *Ta 254* was to be twin *Jumo 213E*, *DB 603E*, or *DB 603L* piston engines. The maximum speed anticipated for the *Ta 254* with twin *Jumo 213E* engines, using *MW 50* boost was estimated to be 460 mph (736 km/h) at 34,500 feet [10,520 meters]. *DB 603* engines were only in the development stage prior to war's end. Only a few specifications of the proposed *Ta 254* are available today and include:

Wing Area: 452 square feet
Weight, Fully Loaded at Take-Off: 25,300 pounds
Speed, Maximum: 424 mph at 34,750 feet altitude
Time to climb to 32,800 feet: 21 minutes
Service Ceiling: 37,700 feet altitude

• *Ta 254Ra-1* - preliminary design for the proposed *Ta 254A* series with three subtypes each powered by twin *Jumo 213E* piston engines turning *VS-19* 4-bladed wooden propellers.
• *Ta 254A-1* - two seat night fighter with a hinged cockpit canopy and ejection seats.
• *Ta 254A-2* - two seat day fighter.
• *Ta 254A-3* - single seat day fighter.
• *Ta 254Ra-2* - preliminary design for the proposed *Ta 254B* series with three subtypes each powered by twin *Daimler-Benz 603L* piston engines turning *VDM* 3-bladed metal propellers.
• *Ta 254B-1* - two seat night fighter similar to the *Ta 154A-1*.
• *Ta 254B-2* - three seat day fighter similar to the *Ta 154A-2*.
• *Ta 254B-3* - single seat day fighter based on the *Ta 154A-3*.

It appears that no *Ta 254* series machines were constructed prior to war's end.

The *Ta 154 A-1* two seat night fighting *Moskito* is victorious over its RAF namesake with the *Mosquito's* starboard engine engulfed in flames. Digital image by *Mario Merino*.

Because of British interest in the structural techniques employed in the *Ta 154* design, it had appeared in Category One Requirements List, and three dismantled *154s* were located and one of them was shipped to RAE-Farnborough. The three machines were found at *Luftpark* (Storage Depot) at Paderborn. As far as it is known to this author only one *Ta 154* was sent to RAE, and it was the subject of an engineering investigation, resulting in the issue of RAE Report EA 262/1. It is not known if a RAF Air Ministry "AirMin" number was assigned to any or all of the three *Ta 154s*.

One very rare fully assembled *Ta 154A-4* two seat night fighter was found post war and brought to the United States in July 1945. It had been loaded on the *Library* ship *SS Richard J. Gatling*. In addition to this *Ta 154A*, the *SS Gatling* carried two *Me 163Bs*, and five sailplanes among them, with several *Horten* all-wing sailplanes. After being unloaded the *Ta 154A* transported to Freeman Field, Indiana, was listed among the exhibits shown at the Institute of Aviation Sciences during the exhibition held at Freeman Field during September 1945. This *Ta 154A* was reported captured by the USAAF's 54th Air Disarmament Squadron, near the village of Lage in slightly damaged condition. This machine no longer exists, and it was probably one of the many German aircraft scrapped about the time of the Korean war when aircraft manufacturing space was needed more by *Fairchild* (at what is now known as O'Hara airfield outside of Chicago) than *Luftwaffe* aircraft specimens. *Fairchild* was manufacturing the *C-119* cargo-carrying airplane.

"The biggest problem and the cancellation of the series production of the *Ta 154*," said *Gotthold Matthias*, "was the destruction of the *Goldmann Werke* glue-making facility at Wuppertal." This destruction

A nose-port side view of the *Ta 154 V1* at *Focke-Wulf's* Langenhagen assembly facilities after its "roll out" on 1 July 1943. Notice the dark camouflaged *VS-9* 3-bladed wooden propellers and propeller hub-cover spinners.

which *Matthias* was referring to occurred during the nights of 20/21 May 1944 by none other than 30 RAF "*Mosquitos*." Seventy-one people were reported killed on the ground, and the production of the one-of-a-kind *Tego-Film* wood glue ceased entirely. The *RLM*, as an alternative solution, required *Dyanmit AG* of Leverkusen-Schlebusch to produce a *Tego-Film*-like wood glue known as *Kaurit*. *Dyanmit* was able to do this, but its quality was very poor due to numerous sabotage actions by 245 Belgian and French prisoners of war at the glue factory. This *Ersatz* (substitute) glue of very poor quality caused many *Ta 154s* to break apart in mid-air, resulting in numerous fatal crashes. The entire *Ta 154* program was canceled by the *RLM* in mid-August 1944. In the end, the *Luftwaffe* received only 7 or 8 production *Ta 154* night-fighter versions: perhaps 4 in June and 4 in July 1944. There were some completed *154s* and numerous unfinished aircraft and aircraft parts. Everything was dismantled—the completed machines as well as those under assembly—for their metal parts to be recycled and the wooden pieces burned as fire wood. Post war the Allies entering German aircraft manufacturing plants failed to find a single *Ta 154* in flight ready condition. The only known complete *Ta 154* located was the one the United States obtained...but it had suffered su-

perficial damage, and it appears that this machine was never test flown postwar. This machine no longer exists, having been scrapped at Wright-Patterson airbase in the early 1950s. Overall, the *Ta 154* is one of the best examples of the death of an entire aircraft type by Allied bombing combined with sabotage action by its *KZ* inmate laborers.

Specifications of the *154A-1*:

- Type: Single or two-seat bad weather and day and night fighter
- Country: Germany
- Manufacturer: *Focke-Wulf*
- Designer:
- Year Constructed: 1943
- Number Constructed: unknown
- Power Plant (three known types): 2x*Junkers Jumo 213E* with 3-speed 2-stage superchargers and induction coolers providing 1,776 horsepower for take-off and 1,320 horsepower cruising at 32,000 feet altitude; 2x*Junkers Jumo 211R*; 2x*Junkers Jumo 211N*.
- Wing Span: 52 feet 6 inches [16 meters]
- Wing Area: 348.9 square feet [32.4 square meters]
- Wing Loading: na
- Wing Aspect Ratio: na
- Length, overall: 41 feet 3 inches [12.6 meters]
- Height: 12 feet 6 inches [3.6 meters]
- Weight, empty: na

- Weight, Loaded (*A-1*): 18,600 pounds [8,445 kilograms]
- Weight, Loaded (*A-2* with *GM-1*): 19,480 pounds [8,845 kilograms]
- Weight, maximum: na
- Fuel, Internal: 396 gallons [1,500 liters]
- Fuel, External: 2x66 gallon drop tanks

- Performance of the *A-1* with twin *Jumo 211N* engines:
- Speed, Maximum: 382 mph [611 lm/h] at 19,000 feet [5,795 meters]
- Climb to 26,240 feet [8,000 meters]: 16 minutes
- Service Ceiling: 31,200 feet [9,520 meters] altitude
- Range, Normal: 890 miles [1,425 kilometers] at 23,000 feet [7,020 meters] altitude
- Range, Maximum with two 66-gallon drop tanks: 1,195 miles [1,912 kilometers] at 23,000 feet [7,020 meters]

- Performance of the *A-1* with twin *Jumo 211B* engines:
- Speed, Maximum: 394 mph [630 km/h] at 26,240 feet [8,000 meters] altitude
- Climb to 26,240 feet [8,000 meters]: 14 1/2 minutes
- Service Ceiling: 35,800 feet [10,920 meters] altitude
- Range, Normal: 855 miles [1,370 kilometers] at 23,000 feet [7,020 meters] altitude
- Range, Maximum with two 66-gallon drop tanks: 1,160 miles [1,860 km] at 23,000 feet [7,020 meters] altitude

- Performance of the *A-2*:
- Speed, Maximum with *GM-1*: 388 mph [621 km/h] at 32,800 feet [10,000 meters] altitude
- Speed, Cruising: na
- Speed, Landing: na
- Take off distance: na
- Time to reach cruising altitude of 26,240 feet: 14 1/2 minutes
- Range, Normal: 855 miles at 23,000 feet altitude
- Range, Maximum: 1,160 miles with the addition of 2x66

gallon drop tanks
- Flight Duration: na
- Service Ceiling: 36,800 feet
- Rate of Climb: na
- Armament: 2x*MK 103* 30 mm cannon with 110 rounds per cannon and 2x*MG 151* 20 mm cannon with 200 rounds per cannon
- Bomb Load: na
- Number Surviving Postwar: 0

Additional details of the *Ta 154* include:

Wings: Shoulder-wing cantilever monoplane. Single-piece wing of all-wood construction attached to the fuselage by four bolts. Straight leading edge. Swept-forward trailing edge carried the ailerons, variable-camber, and slotted flaps. The nacelles, which project beyond the trailing edge were of duralumin, and a lattice bulkhead, located behind the fireproof bulkhead and braced to the rear spar by V-shaped struts, supported the engine and landing gear unit.

Fuselage: All wood oval section structure in one piece from the front bulkhead to the axis of rotation of the rudder. Fin was integral with the fuselage.

Tail Unit: Cantilever monoplane type with a one piece single spar tailplane of light metal construction. Metal-framed and fabric-covered elevators were interchangeable and mass-balanced. Horn-balanced rudder was of similar construction and carried a servo tab which also acted as a trimmer. The tailplane was adjustable in flight around the axis of rotation of the elevators.

Landing Gear: Retractable tricycle type. All wheels retract rearwards, the nose wheel turning through 90 degrees to lie flat in the fuselage. Hydraulic retraction.

Power Plant: Two *Junkers Jumo 211N* or *211R* twelve cylinder inverted V-shaped liquid cooled engines in underslung nacelles with annular nose radiators. Two fuel tanks were located in the fuselage aft of the crew accommodations. Total internal fuel capacity is 330 gallons. An oil tank holding 25 1/2 gallons was located in each engine nacelle.

Pilot Accommodation: Enclosed and armored cockpit in front of leading edge of wings. In two-seat version the radio operator sat behind the pilot facing forward. Entrance to the cabin was through the jettisonable canopy. The cockpit cabin was protected in front by 12 mm armor plating carried on a bulkhead and small side pieces of 8 mm armor plating. The windscreen was 50 mm thick bullet-proof glass with 30 mm thick side panels.

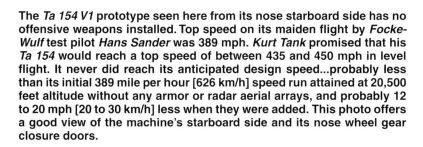

The *Ta 154 V1* prototype seen here from its nose starboard side has no offensive weapons installed. Top speed on its maiden flight by *Focke-Wulf* test pilot *Hans Sander* was 389 mph. *Kurt Tank* promised that his *Ta 154* would reach a top speed of between 435 and 450 mph in level flight. It never did reach its anticipated design speed...probably less than its initial 389 mile per hour [626 km/h] speed run attained at 20,500 feet altitude without any armor or radar aerial arrays, and probably 12 to 20 mph [20 to 30 km/h] less when they were added. This photo offers a good view of the machine's starboard side and its nose wheel gear closure doors.

Armament: 2x*MK 108* 30 mm (110 rounds per cannon) and 2x*MG 151* 20 mm (200 rounds per cannon) in the fuselage sides below the leading-edge of the wings and firing forward. Alternative armament *consisted* of 4x*MK 108* 30 mm or 4x*MG 151* 20 mm cannon. Ammunition boxes for the upper cannon are in the leading edge of the wings between the fuselage and nacelles, and those for the lower cannon are in the fuselage. In addition to the forward-firing cannon, 2x*MG 108* 39 mm fixed cannon firing forward and obliquely-upward could have been installed in the fuselage of the night fighter version.

Ta 154 Werk Nummern, Known Use/Disposition

Werk Nummer	Radio Call Code	Production Model	Known Use/Disposition
Langenhagen *Ta 154* prototype construction			
100001	TE+FE	V1	1st prototype built.
		V1a	Re-engined *V1* with twin *Jumo 211N* and *VS-9* three bladed wooden propellers. Total loss 5 August 1944 inside its hangar at Langenhagen due to bombing attack by U.S. 8th Air Force *B-17s*. 100002 *TE+FF V2* Total loss from bombing at Langenhagen 5 August 1944.
100003	TE+FG	V3	Total loss from bombing at Langenhagen 5 August 1944.
100004	TE+FH	V4	Converted to a two-seat day fighter as prototype for *Ta 154 A-1/R-1*. Crashed 1 June 1944.
100005	TE+FI	V5	Crashed 7 April 1944.
100006	TE+FJ	V6	Given over to Rechlin Flight Test Center 1 June 1944. Disposition unknown.
100007	TE+FK	V7	Total loss at Langenhagen 5 August 1944.
100008	TE+FL	V8	Modified for tests with twin *Jumo 213A-1* engines and *VS-11* three-bladed wooden propellers. Crashed 6 May 1944.
Posen *Ta 154* prototype and series production			
100009	TE+FM	V9	Crashed 18 April 1944.
100010	TE+FN	V10	Modified for tests with twin *Jumo 213A-1* engines and given a lengthened fuselage.
		V11	Stress testing for *154A* series (destroyed).
		V12	Stress testing for *154A* series (destroyed).
		V13	Stress testing for *154A* series (destroyed).
		V14	Scheduled for stress testing for *154C* series but canceled. *General Adolf Galland* and *Oberst Streib* of *NJG* test flew this machine at Berlin, 2 June 1944.

An eye-level view of the *Ta 154 V1* from behind looking forward and supported by screw-jacks. Notice that the hinged cockpit canopy opens to starboard. This machine is parked inside a work shed at Langenhagen. Early July 1943.

	V15		Prototype for *154A-2* series single-seat day fighter.
	V16		Unknown use/disposition believed to be powered by twin *Jumo 213A-1* engines.
	V17		Unknown use/disposition believed to be powered by twin *Jumo 213A-1* engines.
	V18		Unknown use/disposition believed to be powered by twin *Jumo 213A-1* engines.
	V19		Unknown use/disposition believed to be powered by twin *Jumo 213A-1* engines.
	V20		Prototype for *154C-1* series production with twin *Jumo 213A-1* engines.
	V21		Prototype for *154C-2* and *C-3* series production with twin *Jumo 213A-1* engines.

Ta 154 prototype and *A-O* series production

120001	TQ+XA	V22	Fitted with twin *Jumo 213A-1* engines and *VS-9* three-bladed wooden propellers. Total loss at Langenhagen on 5 August 1944.
120002	TQ+XB	V23	Fitted with twin *Jumo 213A-1* engines and *VS-9* three-bladed wooden propellers.
120003	TQ+XC	A-O	Fitted with twin *Jumo 211F* engines and *VS-11* wooden propellers.
120004	TQ+XD	A-O	Modified to an *A-O/U2.*
120005	TQ+XE	A-O	Believed to be fitted with *FuG 220* aerial array and *SN2* radar.
120006		A-O	Unknown use/disposition.
120007		A-O	Unknown use/disposition.
120008		A-O	Unknown use/disposition.
120009		A-O	Scheduled to be powered by twin *Jumo 211R* engines. Unknown if configured as planned and unknown use/disposition.
120010		A-O	Scheduled to be powered by twin *Jumo 211R* engines. Unknown if configured as planned and unknown use/disposition.
120011		A-O/U1	Built initially as an *A-O/U1* then modified to a *A-O/U2* and otherwise unknown.
120012		A-O/U1	Built initially as an *A-O/U1* then modified to an *A-O/U2* and otherwise unknown.
120013		A-O/U1	Unknown use or disposition.
120014		A-O/U1	Unknown use or disposition.
120015		A-O/U1	Unknown use or disposition.
120056		A-O/U1	Unknown use or disposition.
120057		A-O/U1	Unknown use or disposition.
120058		A-O/U1	Unknown use or disposition.
120059		A-O/U1	Unknown use or disposition.
120060		A-O/U1	Built initially as an *A-O/U1* then modified to *an A-O/U2.*
120061		A-O/U1	Unknown use or disposition.
120062		A-O/U1	Unknown use or disposition.
120063		A-O/U1	Unknown use or disposition.
120064		A-O/U1	Built initially as an *A-O/U1* then modified to an *A-O/U2.*

Erfurt - *Ta 154A-1, A-2,* and *A-4* series production

320001	KU+SN	A-1	Unknown if completed, use or disposition.
320002	KU+SO	A-1	Crashed/destroyed on 28 June 1944.
320003	KU+SP	A-1	Unknown if completed, use or disposition.
320004	KU+SQ	A-1	Crashed/destroyed on 16 June1944.
320005	KU+SR	A-1	Unknown if completed, use or disposition.
320006	KU+SS	A-1	Unknown if completed, use or disposition.
320007	KU+ST	A-4	Crashed/destroyed on 28 June 1944.
320008	KU+SU (D5+HR)	A-4	Crashed/destroyed on 30 April 1945.
320009	KU+SV	A-2	Unknown if completed, use or disposition.
320010	KU+SW	A-2	Unknown if completed, use or disposition.
320011		A-2	Crashed/destroyed on 28 September 1944.
320012			Unknown version, use or disposition.
320058			Unknown version, use or disposition.
320059		A-2	Unknown if completed, use or disposition.

Notes:
A-O - pre-production two seat night fighter versions.
A-O/U1 - "*U1*" meaning umrüst-bausätze or a pre-production construction modification #1.
A-O/U2 - "*U2*" meaning umrüst-bausätze or a pre-production construction modification #2.
A-1 - two-seat day fighter.
A-2 - single-seat night fighter.
A-3 - two-seat trainer.
A-4 - two-seat night fighter (limited production prior to series cancellation) with upturned wing tips to give dihedral and *FuG 212A* and *FuG 220* radar.
Ra-1 - "*Ra*" meaning "*raffinat*" or refinement.

The *Ta 154 V1* has been parked out on the tarmac, and it is being viewed from behind with a good view of its full-span tailplane elevators. The *V1's* long-length oleo nose gear made the prototype appear as if it was a "tail dragger." This oleo strut was changed to a full castoring version beginning with the *V3.*

A direct nose-on view of the *Ta 154 V1.* Notice its rectangular nose wheel gear door. From this angle, too, it appears that this *Moskito* was a "tail dragger," but it really wasn't.

A nose on view of the *Ta 154 V1* two seat night fighter at Langenhagen. This machine appears with a nose-mounted *FuG 212* radar aerial array. It may have its fuselage-mounted cannon installed, too. Its camouflage scheme is not readily apparent in this twilight-taken photo.

Shown in this photo is a scale model of the prototype *Ta 154 A-4* night-fighter. Its upper surface would have had camouflage *74 Gray-Green*, *75 Gray-Violet*, while its under surface would have been *76 Light Blue*. Courtesy *Flugzeug 1/88*.

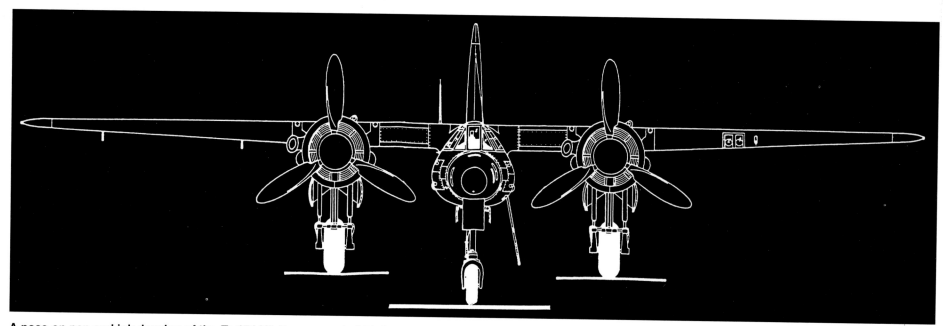

A nose-on pen and ink drawing of the *Ta 154 V1*. Nose-mounted *FuG* radar aerial arrays have yet to be installed on this prototype. Courtesy *Karo-As Models*.

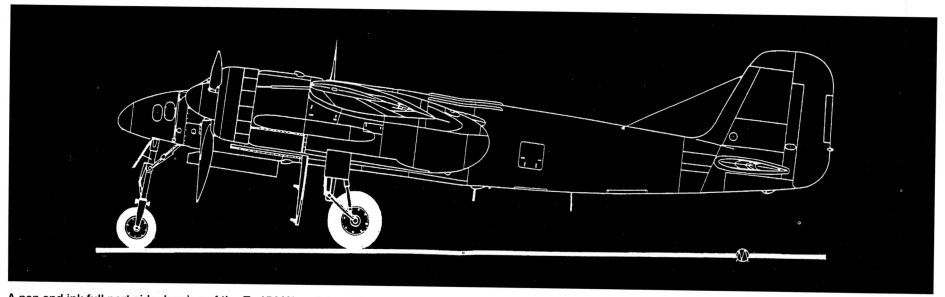

A pen and ink full port side drawing of the *Ta 154 V1* prototype. Cannon were not installed for its maiden flight and high speed testing. Courtesy *Karo-As Models*.

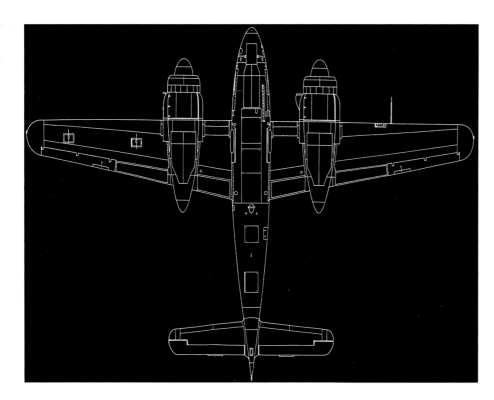

A full-view upper surface of the *Ta 154 V1* prototype is featured in this pen and ink drawing. The parallel bars seen running length-wise on the upper fuselage aft of the wing's trailing edge were added to stiffen the fuselage. Courtesy *Karo-As Models*.

A pen and ink illustration featuring a full-view of the underside of the *Ta 154 V1* prototype. Courtesy *Karo-As Models*.

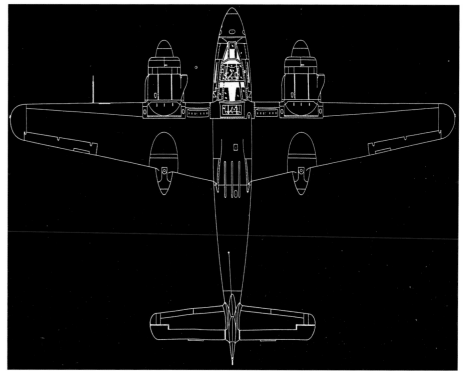

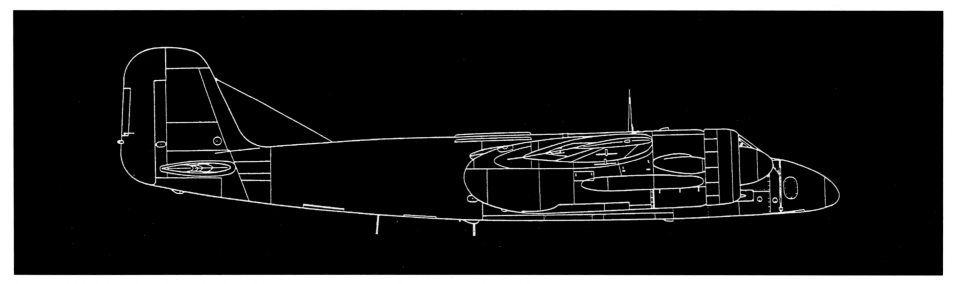

A pen and ink full starboard side drawing of the *Ta 154 V1* prototype. Courtesy *Karo-As Models*.

A cut-away pen and ink view of a fully equipped *Ta 154 A-4* with the older *FuG 212* radar aerial array. Courtesy *E. Mayer and AIRPOWER Magazine*, 11/1988.

An aerial RAF reconnaissance photo of the city of Lübeck the morning after its 28 March 1942 incendiary bomb night attack by Bomber Command. The areas circled in white have been burned out due to incendiary bombs creating intense fires.

An aerial RAF reconnaissance photo of the city of Rostock the morning after its incendiary bombing by Bomber Command in early April 1942. Visible at the top and bottom of the photo are large areas of the city destroyed by fire...some areas still smoking.

Piles of smoking rubble the morning after the RAF's night raid on the city of Rostock and nearby *Ernst Heinkel AG.*

An ill-fated RAF *Avro "Manchester"* bomber is shown in the process of dropping its load of incendiary bombs. Only used between February 1941 and June 1942, these twin engine bombers were the RAF's biggest disappointments of WWII and only 209 machines were constructed. They were a disappointment because they were unable to achieve their design specifications. Many "*Manchesters*" were lost on bombing raids into Germany.

This is how a fire-bombed German city looked from the air at night following a RAF raid of incendiary bombs. Fires have started everywhere and are illuminating the night sky for miles around.

A view at "ground zero" of a German city set aflame at night by RAF bombers. Early efforts by *Luftwaffe* night fighters and *flak* guns were only able to bring down about 4% of the attackers on any given night. A 4% loss rate would mean, on average, a complete squadron crew turnover about every four months due to shoot downs. Bad for Bomber Command, but not anywhere good enough for Germany when their bomb loads consisted mainly of incendiary bombs whose sole purpose was to set fire to populated urban areas.

The railroad marshaling yards in Cologne before the 1,046 RAF bomber raid directed by Bomber Command Director *Arthur "Bomber" Harris.*

The same Cologne railroad yards the morning after the 1,046 RAF bomber raid on 30 May 1942. Actually, only 898 RAF bombers reached Cologne...148 missed the target or turned back due to mechanical problems. RAF night bombers have left the Cologne railroad yards pretty well unusable for months.

A typical *Luftwaffe Flak 36* battery with its single 88 mm cannon pointed skyward to Allied heavy bombers. But *Boeing B-17s* and *Avro Lancasters*, for example, were tough birds, and it often required a direct hit to bring them down. The 88mm 36 flak shells could reach an altitude of 25,000 feet, and a well-trained crew could fire off between 15 and 20 rounds per minute.

"My name is *Hermann Göring*, but if ever a single bomb should manage to fall on German soil then you can call me *Myer*." Despite the bombs raining down on Germany during its five-year struggle, it appears that *Göring's* popularity among the citizens of the *Reich* remained high and that he could still go out and about conversing with survivors right up to war's end without fear of being attacked himself. *Göring* is shown here about 1944.

A battery of German 88 mm anti-aircraft guns (*Flak 36's*) being fired at night against RAF bombers.

Generalmajor Josef Kammhuber...boss of the night fighters until he was fired by *Hitler* and sent into exile in Norway by *Hermann "Myer" Göring*.

A *Bf 110C* early version night fighter belonging to *3./NJG.1* and shown before airborne radar. These early night fighter pilots had to pick out RAF bombers through visual contact. The *110C* is camouflaged in black except for its "*Kauz I,*" or Screech Owl #1, unit emblem in white.

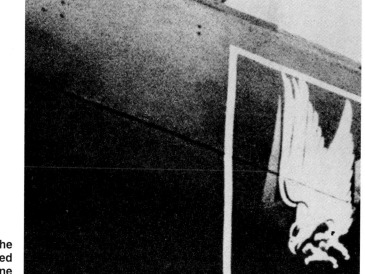

The port side of a *Do 17Z-10* showing the emblem "*Kauz I,*" or Screech Owl #1, of the *Luftwaffe's NJG.1.* The pilot of this night-fighting machine is *Hauptmann Ludwig Becker...Staffelkapitän* of *4./NJG.1.* He is credited in obtaining the first night-fighter victory through the use of radar, in this case the initial *FuG 202* airborne radar system. He was killed in action on 26 February 1943 after having achieved 45 kills. A huge loss to the night fighters.

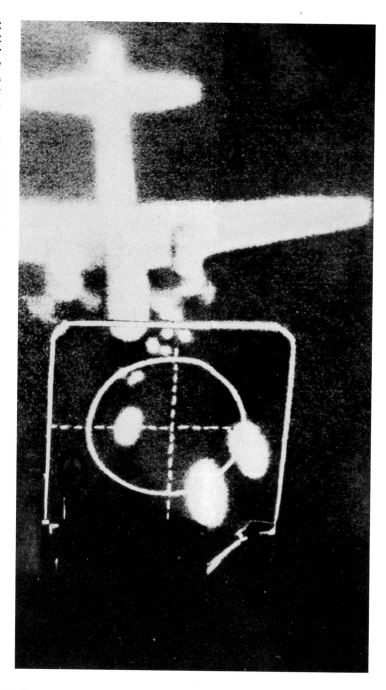

Left: An early *NJG.1* pilot following a RAF bomber at night through his reflector gunsight. This was how these night-fighter pilots made contract with enemy bombers before radar was installed in their machines. A very difficult, awkward, and dangerous way of seeking out enemy bombers over German skies. The danger was double because *Flak 36* batteries on the ground were firing away, too, all seeking the same RAF bomber.

A photo of cannon fire from a *NJG.1* night-fighter cutting into the starboard wing of a RAF bomber as seen through its reflector gunsight.

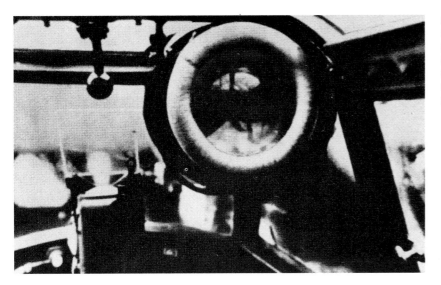

A hoped for improvement in the crude reflector gunsight was the *NJG.1*'s so-called "*spanner anlage*" system. This night vision device shown here in a *Bf 110C* was an infra-red (IR) scope and was to identify enemy bombers by their heat emitting from the engine(s) exhaust and displaying information on a "Q *tube*" in the cockpit. In effect, the *spanner anlage* IR was an attempt to turn night into day. At short ranges it did show some value but it was not good enough to be effective in destroying RAF bombers to the point that Bomber Command would give up their night bombing raids over Germany.

A rare *Do 17* known as the *Z-7* equipped with the round pipe-like infra-red "*spanner anlage*" device extending through its windshield. It was hoped that this *Z-7* would overcome the disadvantages of the *Bf 110*. It did not and pilot's still relied on eye contact "cat's eye" aided by those huge 5 foot [152 centimeter] diameter search lights on the ground to spot enemy bombers. This practice was known as "*Helle Nachtjagd*" or illuminated night fighting.

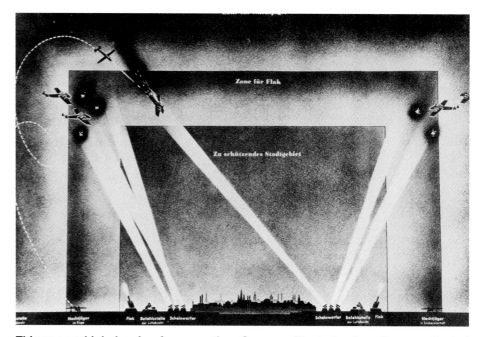

This pen and ink drawing from war-time Germany illustrates how the complicated use of night-fighters, *flak 36* guns, and search lights were suppose to work in bring down RAF heavy bombers. Surrounding a German city were *flak* guns and search lights which is represented by the small box/zone in the center of the drawing. The box immediately above is the *flak* zone which is also illuminated by search lights. The top box/zone is where German night fighters operated...above the *flak* zone...whereby roving night fighter pilots relied on the searchlights to reveal the enemy RAF bombers and then on their "cat's eyes" to achieve the shoot-down.

A *Luftwaffe* searchlight crew with their 5 foot [152 centimeter] diameter light scanning the night skies for enemy bombers as a light rain is falling.

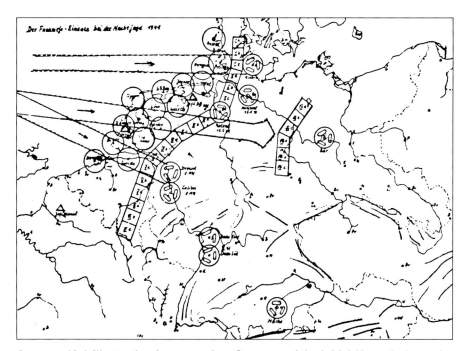

Der Funkmeß-Einsatz bei der Nachtjagd 1941

A pen and ink illustration from war-time Germany of the initial *Kammhuber* radar aerial defensive line. On the left are lines and arrows representing RAF bombers coming from across the English Channel. Circles represent *Luftwaffe* fighter zones. Behind them are squares representing areas of search lights where illuminated night fighting or of *NJG.1* took place.

The practice of *Helle Nachtjagd* was soon replaced by the advent of ground radar in the form of *Telefunken's Freya (FuMG 80)* early warning radar antenna. Information collected was sent to the night fighter and displayed on a cathode screen in the cockpit via *Telefunken's FuG 202* airborne radar scope from its "mattress bedspring" aerial array. This early German radar was crude and unreliable but it worked and its range was gradually extended to over two miles and so too its reliability. To the right in the photo is one of the many *Freya* stacked ground radar arrays located along the French coast. To the left is the newer *Würzburg-Riese* radar dish. Each was used and maintained by *Kammhuber's* night-fighting organization. The *Freya* radar was a long range search radar picking up the RAF bombers as they were leaving England. After RAF bombers had been located one of the two *Würzburg-Riese* radar dishes tracked the heavy bombers, while a second *Würzburg-Riese* radar dish tracked the *Luftwaffe* night fighter. Position information from the *Würzburg-Riese* radars was then handed off to the *flak* command post where the information was evaluated and displayed on a horizontal glass table-top, or "*Seeburg Table*." Red and green points of light shown down by a number of female plotters from bleachers above, indicated the positions of RAF bombers and *Luftwaffe* night fighters. When *Kammhuber* was fired and sent to exile in Norway and replaced by *Generalmajor* "*Beppo*" *Schmid*, the practice of radar guided night-fighters which *Kammhuber* had established fell pretty much into disuse.

Shown in this photo is a close-up view of the large diameter *Würzburg-Riese* radar dish used to track incoming RAF night-flying bombers traveling to Germany from England. A second *Würzburg-Riese* dish tracked *Luftwaffe* night fighters guiding them to the bomber formations. With this system the three zones of the initial *Kammhuber* line of illuminated search lights, *flak* guns, and night fighters seeking out the RAF bombers through visual contact didn't work all that well and it gave way to radar identified RAF heavy bombers. From this time on, *Luftwaffe* night fighters would be guided by radar to the enemy bombers.

A *Do 217N-2* with its *FuG 202* AI antenna "barbed wire or mattress bedspring" aerial array mounted on its fuselage nose. This photo is from late 1942.

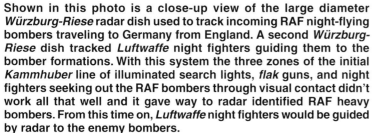

The *Lichtenstein BC* airborne *FuG 202* radar's "mattress bedspring" aerial array initially used by *Kammhuber*'s *NJG.1* pilots and shown in this photo mounted on one of their *Bf 110C* night fighters.

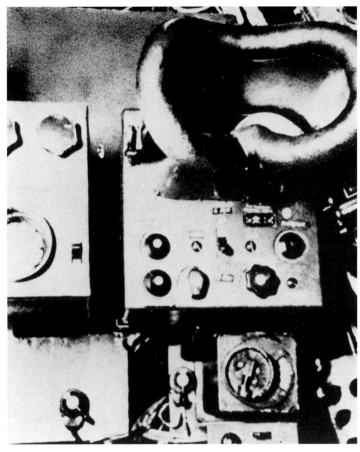

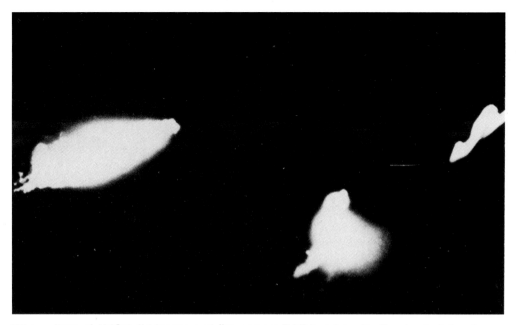

When pilots of *NJG.1* did locate and fire upon a RAF bomber...it often broke into pieces. Shown in this photo is a RAF night bomber which has broken into three pieces, each piece on fire, and falling to earth.

The rubber boot a radio/radar operator looked into to see the *FuG 202's* three individual round radar scopes showing distance, vertical, and horizontal measurements.

The remains of a RAF twin engine *Vickers Supermarine "Wellington"* bomber on German soil the morning after a night bombing raid.

A RAF four engine *Handley-Page "Halifax"* heavy bomber the morning after night bombing mission over Germany.

An RAF twin engine *Vickers Supermarine "Wellington"* bomber the morning after being shot down in the night by night-fighters from *Kammhuber's NJG.1.*

A dead RAF bomber crew member lies on German soil the morning after a bombing raid which brought him and his aircraft down.

Former RAF bomber crew members being held in a German prisoner of war (POW) camp attest to the successful efforts put forth by *Kammhuber* and members of his *NJG.1*. Even though the number of men shown in this photo appears large, they represented only a small fraction of the total number of RAF bombers attacking Germany without being touched by the night fighters and *flak* guns.

This early non-radar version *Bf 110* night fighter was forced down after taking cannon fire from a RAF "*Halifax*" or "*Lancaster*" bomber over Cologne.

A *FuG 202* radar aerial array equipped *Bf 110* night fighter was forced down during the night as a result of cannon fire. Radar equipped or not, RAF bomber crew fought the night fighters with great intensity.

Göring, Kammhuber, and *Hauptmann Manfred Meuer. Meuer* was *Kommandeur* of the night fighter group *1 Staffel of Nachtjagdgeschwader (NJG)1* and was killed in action on 21 January 1944. Behind *Göring* and barely seen is his fellow pilot from World War I, friend, and then Head of *Luftwaffe* Personnel...*Generaloberst Bruno Lorzer.*

This is what *Kammhuber* wanted to equip his entire *NJG.1* with...the *Heinkel He 219* night fighter. It was not meant to be. Fitted out with *Daimler-Benz 603A* engines, *FuG 220* radar aerial arrays, and flame dampers, this machine was capable of 364 mph [585 km/h] forward speed...faster than any other night-fighting flying machine The *He 219* shown in this photo is presently in storage at the National Air & Space Museum, Silver Hill, Maryland awaiting restoration. It carries Foreign Equipment (FE) number 612 where it can be seen at the bottom of its starboard tail fin.

A nose starboard side view of the *Heinkel He 219 V18* which featured experimental four bladed propellers and powered by twin *Jumo 222A/B* engines although the *He 219* in this photo has *V5* painted on its nose. The *He 219 V1* had made its maiden flight on 15 November 1941. Normally the *He 219* was powered by twin *Daimler-Benz 603A* engines of 1,750 hp at take-off.

This was *Junkers'* entry into *Oberst Knemeyer's* night fighter competition...the three-seat *Ju 388K*. Only four examples are known to this author to have been constructed and all were powered by twin *BMW 801TJ* radial piston engines with exhaust-driven turbo superchargers. The *Ju 388K* was similar to the *Ju 88*, however, it carried 2x*MG 131* 13 mm cannon and a bomb load of 6,610 pounds.

Generalfeldmarshall Erhard Milch was skeptical about the *He 219*, the *Me 410*, and the proposed *Ju 388* as replacements for the exiting crop of night fighters such as the *Do 17*, *Ju 88*, and the *Bf 110*. In the end he chose to increase the number of *Bf 110s* as the immediate solution, the *Ju 88* as the interim solution, and the *Ju 388* as the long-range solution. A *Ju 188* without bomb racks, radar, and cannon was shown to be 19 mph [30 km/h] faster than a fully equipped *He 219*. Plus flight tests of the *He 219* showed that it was about 10 mph [16 km/h] less than *Ernst Heinkel AG* had promised, inadequate stability around its yaw axis, and vibration in its tail assembly.

Milch didn't want the *He 219* as did *Kammhuber*, nevertheless, *Milch* ordered more *Bf 110s* for the night fighters. Shown in this photo are four *Bf 110 G-2/R3s* closing in on a day-light Allied bomber formation over Germany in 1943.

Radar equipped German night fighters became less and less effective as a result of RAF counter measures. In this photo, it appears that RAF intelligence officers examining one of *Kammhuber's Würzburg-Riese* ground-based radar dishes.

A major blow to the night fighters came in May 1943 and then again in July 1943. On 9 May 1943 the crew of radar equipped *Ju 88 D5+EV* of *4.NJG3* defected to Britain from Aalberg and was escorted in by RAF *Spitfires* from 165 Squadron. This *Ju 88* is presently in the RAF Museum. On 13 July 1943 the RAF obtained a second even newer radar equipped *Ju 88G-1* night fighter. This came about as a result of *Ju 88G-1 4R+UR* of *7.NJG2* landing at the RAF airfield at Woodbridge in Suffolk, England after becoming lost over Holland in their effort to fly east to Germany from Holland. The inexperienced crew becoming disoriented in the darkness mistakenly flew a reciprocal compass heading (west) instead. The loss to the *Luftwaffe* was substantial. The *Ju 88G-1* carried the latest *FuG 220 Lichtenstein SN-2* and the *FuG 227 "Flensburg"* homing device. The *FuG 227* was a device which allowed the night fighters to home in to the RAF *Monica* transmissions that a German night fighter was closing in up behind them. It was a transmitter located in the tail of RAF bombers and was accurate from 3,000 feet to 4 miles. The RAF suddenly learned why their losses were so heavy. The RAF flew the *Ju 88G-1* in a series of tests to determine its twin radar's weaknesses and strengths. *Thus* with a host of countermeasures by the RAF. The *FuG 220 SN-2* was rendered useless by making the RAF's metal foil "window" longer than they had been using. The *FuG 227* also became useless because the RAF removed them from their bombers because they had no immediate way of counteracting this very fine and very accurate German radar. Shown in this photo is the *Ju 88G* which defected on 9 May 1943.

Most of *Kammhuber's* early warning radar stations along the coast of France were bombed out of operation like this one which appears to have included a *Freya* and *Würzburg-Riese* radars.

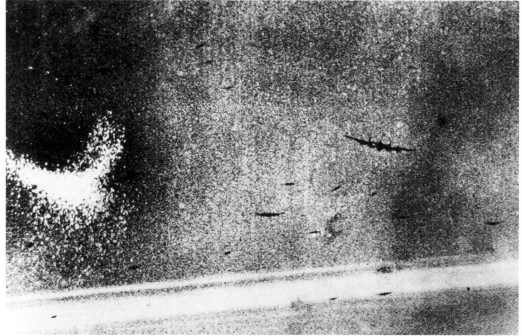

Another item which helped compromised *Kammhuber's* radar network and neutralizing his night fighters was the RAF's discovery that the metal foil "*window*" which they had been using had to be bit longer. When it was lengthened clouds of aluminum metal foil strips which confused the *FuG 220 SN-2* radar. Shown in this photo is the RAF's "window" on the left appearing in white. To the right of the photo is a lone RAF bomber.

Unable to immediately counter the RAF's longer metal foil "*Window*" meant the end to the *FuG 220, FuG 227,* and *Kammhuber.* Shown in this photo is a farewell party given for *Kammhuber* following his firing by *Hilter* and sent into exile in Norway by *Göring.* Left to right is *Kammhuber, Beppo Schmid, Kammhuber's* replacement, and *General Kurt von Döring,* chief of the *RLM's* Inspection of Fighters Command.

Oberst Hajo Herrmann, former bomber "driver." As a *major, Herrmann* had formed the first *Geschwader* intended to carry out "*Wilde Sau*" or wild pig night-fighting operations with *Bf 109s* against RAF bomber formations.

Generalleutnant Josef "*Beppo*" *Schmid* new head of the night fighters. *Kammhuber's* successor shown visiting one of *Oberst Hajo Herrmann's* "*Wilde Sau*" squadrons.

A *Bf 109* night fighter belonging to *Oberst Hajo Herrmann*. Despite all the bravo, *Luftwaffe* fighter pilots were unaccustomed to night time flying nor had they been trained much for these types of fighter operations and the pilots did not achieve many RAF bomber kills. Usually, the night fighting pilot was lost attempting to land in the dark frequently miles away from their home base.

A pen and ink drawing illustrating the "*Wilde Sau*" operation featuring a *Bf 109G* in pursuit of RAF heavy bombers. In the center of the photo is an insert showing the boar's head emblem of *Oberst Hajo Herrmann's* "*Wilde Sau*" night fighters.

Right: *Kurt Tank* and *Ludwig Mittelhüber* shown working on the design of their *Ta 154*. *Mittelhüber* was head of *Focke-Wulf's* aircraft planning department. Both men took advantage of a post-war offer by *Juan Perón* to come to Argentina and construct *Han's Muthopp's Ta 183* proposed jet fighter design there under bomber less skies. The machine was called the *Pulqui II*.

Oberst Siegfried Knemeyer and proudly wearing his knight's cross. Post war he was invited to the United States along with many German scientists via *Operation Paperclip.* He spent most of his working career at Wright-Patterson Air Force Base, Dayton, Ohio. *Knemeyer* was awarded the Distinguished Civilian Service award in 1966 and died at Springfield, Ohio on 11 April 1976 at 70 years of age.

The so-called *KB 303* version (1943) of the *de Havilland Mosquito.* It could reach 34,000 feet altitude and a level forward speed in excess of 400 mph powered by its twin *Rolls-Royce* "*Merlin*" engines. This model shown has a plexiglass nose...it is an early bomber model. The *Mosquito* had a pressurized cockpit cabin equal to 5,000 feet altitude.

A *Mosquito* equipped with 60 pound heads on wing-mounted rocket projectiles, eight of them in racks, hard over a target on a short-range tactical air strike.

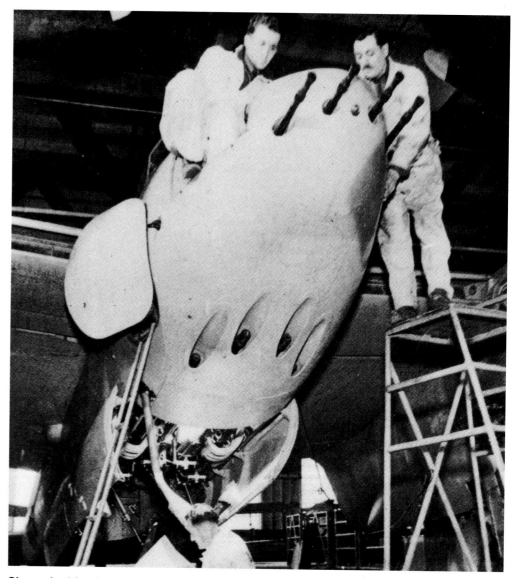

Shown in this photo is the fighter version of the RAF's *Mosquito*. Mounted in the upper portion of its nose were *4xBrowning* machine guns while in the lower portion were 4x20mm cannon.

Shown in this photo is a early wind tunnel model of *Kurt Tank's* twin engine German version of the RAF *Mosquito* and known as the *Ta 154 Moskito*. Notice that the dorsal surface of the fuselage did not cover the entire wing as it did on later production models.

A port side view of the early wind tunnel model of *Kurt Tank's Ta 154*.

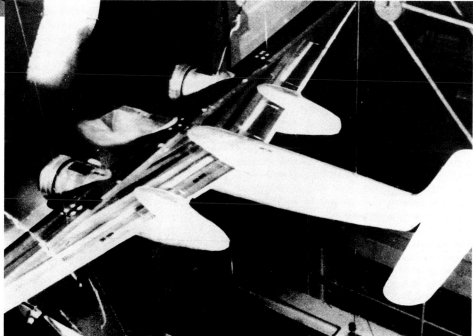

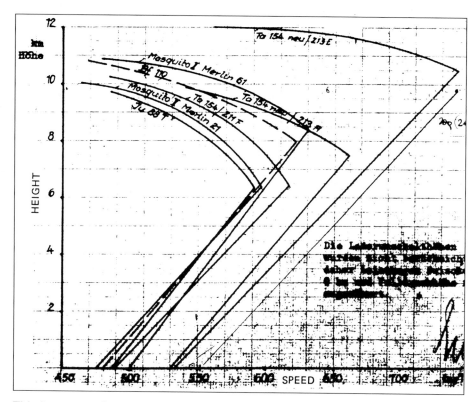

This is a copy of a graphic comparison by *Focke-Wulf* from *WWII* comparing their *Ta 154* to the *de Havilland Mosquito*. *Focke-Wulf's Ta 154* (powered by twin *Jumo 213E* engines with a two-stage, three-speed supercharger providing a rated take-off horsepower of 1,750) was projected to reach a higher altitude than *de Havilland's Mosquito* and obtain in excess of 466 mph [750 km/h] compared to the *Mosquito* and is top speed of in excess of 404 mph [650 km/h]. Were the *Ta 154* to be powered by twin *Jumo 213A* engines the machine would out-speed the *Mosquito* but its surface ceiling would be less. The *Ta 154* never obtained this anticipated speed.

A poor quality photo of a wind tunnel model of the *Ta 154 V-1*. It appears that this is a latter wind tunnel version and closer to the final design because the upper fuselage now extends over the entire wing and the model is shown with a *FuG 212 C-1* "mattress bedspring" aerial radar array on its nose.

A poor quality photo of a wind tunnel scale model of the *Ta 154 V-1* seen from its port side. This scale model appears to be the final wind tunnel design version of the *Moskito*.

This image is thought to be the final wind tunnel version of the *Ta 154 V-1* as seen from its nose port side. Notice how the fuselage extends across the entire width of the wing. Digital image by *Mario Merino*.

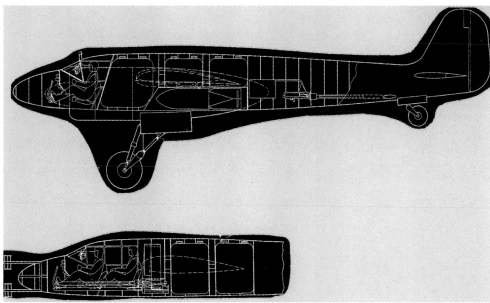

A pen and ink *Focke-Wulf* drawing from 14 October 1942 of their proposed *Ta 154 V-1*. Two versions are presented: a tail-dragging single-seat, fast bomber powered by *2xJumo 211F* engines. The second version is a two seat night fighter carrying a *FuG 212 C-1* "mattress bedspring" radar array and also powered by *2xJumo 211F* engines. The *Jumo 211F* had a take-off horsepower rating of 1,340 verses 1,750 for the *Jumo 213E*.

A scale model by *Focke-Wulf Flugzeug* of what appears to be a final version of the *Ta 154* as seen from its nose port side.

A nose on view of the fuselage and port side engine nacelle wooden mock up of the *Ta 154 V-1* for review by *Oberst Siegfried Knemeyer* and others from the *RLM*.

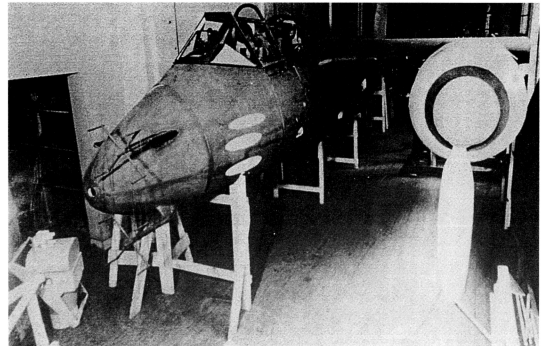

Another nose port side view of *Focke-Wulf's* wooden mockup of their *Ta 154 V-1.* Notice that in the lower left corner of the photograph is a reconnaissance camera. Perhaps *Focke-Wulf* was also telling the *RLM* that their *Ta 154* could be fashioned as a reconnaissance aircraft, too. It is also interesting that only one wood-carved *VS-11* 3-wooden blade propeller is attached while in the above photo all three blades are shown. On its nose is featured a *FuG 212 C-1* radar aerial array.

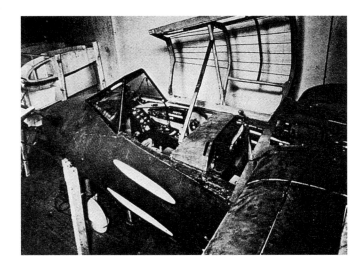

An overhead view of *Focke-Wulf's* wooden *Ta 154 V-1* mockup. The twin rectangular white areas are the cannon muzzle blast troughs/ports. Notice that a pair of wings appear in the upper left hand corner of the photo. This author does not know to what aircraft they belong or why they are included in the area of the mockup. The *154 V-1's* one piece cockpit canopy is hinged and opens to starboard allowing both the pilot and radio/radar operator access to their seats.

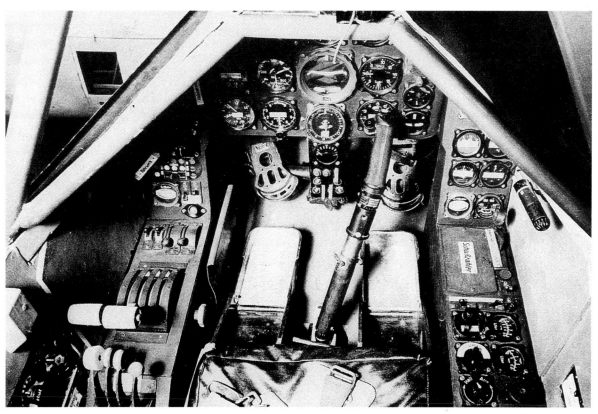

The proposed pilot's cockpit area of the *Ta 154* as seen in the wooden mockup.

The wooden mockup of the *Ta 154* featuring the radio/radar person's cockpit aft of the pilot's seat. The arrangement of radio and radar equipment appears to have been changed from the arrangement shown in the previous photo. It is not known to this author if this version was the first, second, or a later one.

The proposed cockpit from the *Ta 154's* wooden mockup as seen from radio/radar operator's position.

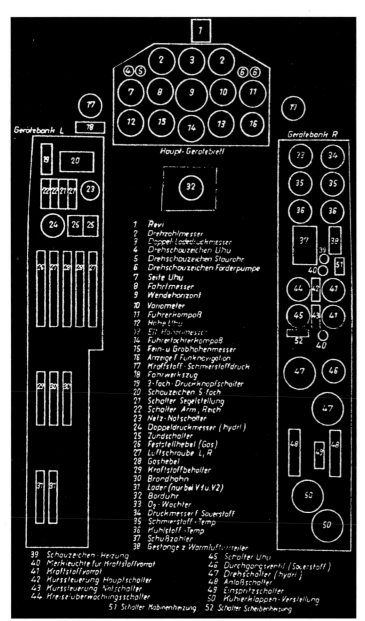

Gerätebank L

Haupt-Gerätebrett

Gerätebank R

1 Revi
2 Drehzahlmesser
3 Doppel-Ladedruckmesser
4 Drehschauzeichen Uhu
5 Drehschauzeichen Staurohr
6 Drehschauzeichen Förderpumpe
7 Seite Uhu
8 Fahrtmesser
9 Wendehorizont
10 Variometer
11 Führerkompaß
12 Höhe Uhu
13 Elt Höhenmesser
14 Führertochterkompaß
15 Fein-u Grobhöhenmesser
16 Anzeige f Funknavigation
17 Kraftstoff-Schmierstoffdruck
18 Fahrwerkszug
19 3-fach-Druckknopfschalter
20 Schauzeichen 5-fach
21 Schalter Segelstellung
22 Schalter Arm, Reich
23 Netz-Notschalter
24 Doppeldruckmesser (hydr)
25 Zündschalter
26 Feststellhebel (Gas)
27 Luftschraube L, R
28 Gashebel
29 Kraftstoffbehälter
30 Brandhahn
31 Lader (nur bei V1 u.V2)
32 Borduhr
33 O₂-Wächter
34 Druckmesser f Sauerstoff
35 Schmierstoff-Temp
36 Kühlstoff-Temp
37 Schußzähler
38 Gestänge z Warmluftverteiler

39 Schauzeichen-Heizung
40 Merkleuchte für Kraftstoffvorrat
41 Kraftstoffvorrat
42 Kurssteuerung Hauptschalter
43 Kurssteuerung Notschalter
44 Kreiselüberwachungsschalter
45 Schalter Uhu
46 Durchgangsventil (Sauerstoff)
47 Drehschalter (hydr)
48 Anlaßschalter
49 Einspritzschalter
50 Kühlerklappen-Verstellung
51 Schalter Kabinenheizung
52 Schalter Scheibenheizung

A pen and ink diagram by *Focke-Wulf Flugzeug* of the pilot's cockpit instruments, switches, levers, and so on proposed for the *Ta 154* in their wooden mockup.

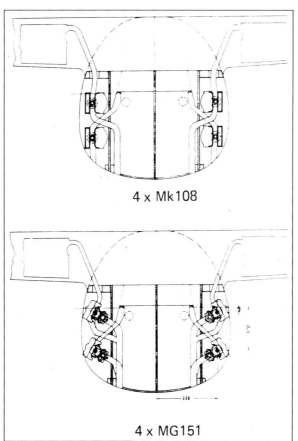

4 x Mk108

4 x MG151

In other versions *Focke-Wulf* was telling the *RLM* that their *Ta 154 V-1* could be equipped with *4xMK 108* cannon or *4xMG 151* cannon as shown in this pen and ink drawing.

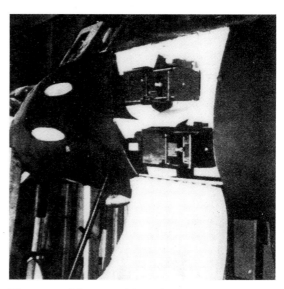

The port side open hinged weapons panel on *Focke-Wulf's 154 V-1* wooden mockup. Several combinations were planned but on this mockup it appears that *Focke-Wulf* was seeking to sell their *Ta 154* with *2xMK 108* 30mm (110 rounds per cannon) lower port and *2xMG 151* 20mm (200 rounds per cannon) upper port. The chute for spent casings was director below the lower cannon.

The prototype *Ta 154 V1* under construction at Langenhagen and featuring the machine's plywood-formed nose port side. The aircraft is being supported by screw jacks. The oblong access port which appears aft of the nose gear is for adjusting the nose wheel retraction mechanism. There was a *similar* port on the opposite side. The uncovered rectangular areas appearing below the cockpit is where the two individual cannon troughs/ports were located: upper for its *MG 151* and lower for its *MK 108* cannon. A good view of the nose wheel leg door and nose wheel door can be seen. The cockpit windscreen featured 50 mm armored glass.

A full starboard side view of the *Ta 154 V1's* fuselage under construction and nearing completion at *Focke-Wulf Flugzeug*-Langenhagen. The nose wheel assembly can be seen on the far left of the photo.

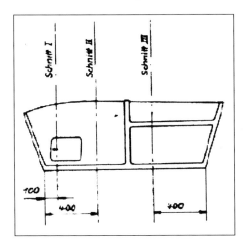

Right: A close up view of what appears to be the cockpit canopy for a *Ta 154* with wooden templates to determine its accuracy according to design plans.

Left: A pen and ink drawing of the *Ta 154's* one-piece cockpit canopy showing its overall length and divided into three cross-sections.

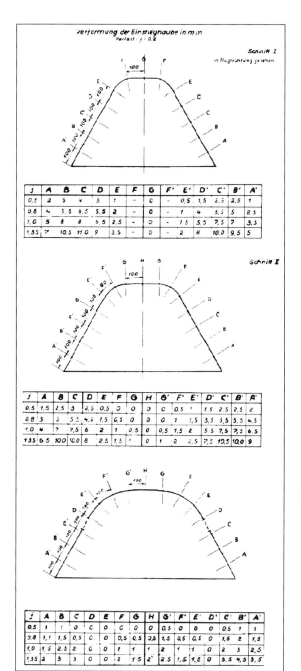

Verformung der Einstieghaube in mm
Verlust f = 0,2

Schnitt I — in Flugrichtung gesehen

j	A	B	C	D	E	F	G	F'	E'	D'	C'	B'	A'
0,5	2	3	4	3	1	-	0	-	0,5	1,5	2,5	2,5	1
0,8	4	5,5	6,5	5,5	2	-	0	-	1	4	5,5	5	2,5
1,0	5	8	8	6,5	2,5	-	0	-	1,5	5,5	7,5	7	3,5
1,35	7	10,5	11,0	9	3,5	-	0	-	2	8	10,0	9,5	5

Schnitt II

j	A	B	C	D	E	F	G	H	G'	F'	E'	D'	C'	B'	A'
0,5	1,5	2,5	3	2,5	0,5	0	0	0	0	0,5	1	1,5	2,5	2,5	2
0,8	3	5	5,5	4,5	1,5	0,5	0	0	1	1,5	3,5	3,5	5,5	5,5	4,5
1,0	4	7	7,5	6	2	1	0,5	0	0,5	1,5	2	5,5	7,5	7,5	6,5
1,35	6,5	10,0	10,0	8	2,5	1,5	1	0	1	2	2,5	7,5	10,5	10,0	9

j	A	B	C	D	E	F	G	H	G'	F'	E'	D	C'	B	A'
0,5	1	0	0	0	0	0	0	0	0,5	0	0	0	0,5	1
0,8	1,1	1,5	0,5	0	0	0,5	0,5	0,5	0,5	0,5	1,5	2	1
1,0	1,5	2,5	2	0	0	1	1	2	1	1	0	2	3	2,5
1,35	2	3	0	0	2	1,5	2	2,5	1,5	1,5	0	3,5	4,5	3,5

While the prototype was being constructed, *Focke-Wulf* engineers built a one-to-one scale nose section to test its aerodynamics. In the Spring of 1943 it was pulled through the water on Lake Alatsee near Füssen in Bavaria. The *Luftfahrt-Forschungsstelle Graf Zeppelin* had perfected a system of underwater drag-testing to determine the strength factor of aircraft structures. In the photo the *Ta 154's* nose and cockpit section has been brought in for inspection.

A pen and ink drawing by section featuring the changing size and shape of the *Ta 154's* cockpit canopy.

Lake Alatsee. It appears that the forward portion of the *Ta 154* including the entire cockpit length and wing stubs is being slowly being placed into the water from its barge via a cable/rope.

Above: A close up of the *Ta 154's* smooth wooden nose as it was being lifted out of Lake Alatsee showing its thick towing/lifting cable/rope.

Left: Lake Alatsee. The *Ta 154's* fuselage/cockpit portion is seen being taken out of the water after a towing test. Notice that the cockpit has what appears to be strips of shipping tape applied and that panels have been broken...either while dragging it through the water or as it was being lifted out.

Left: Lake Alatsee. The port side of the *Ta 154* showing the damaged wing stub. It is not known to this author if the damage occurred while undergoing water testing or as it was being lifted out.

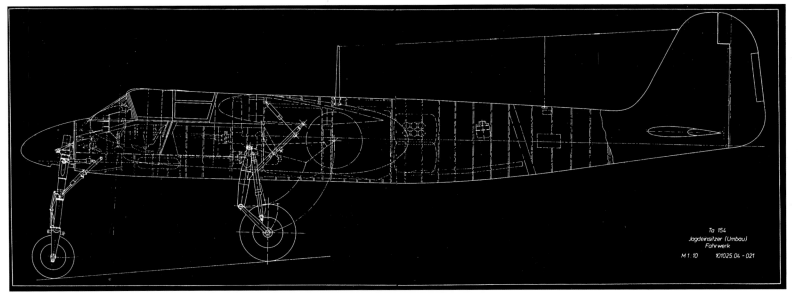

A pen and ink drawing of the *Ta 154 A-O* from *WWII* featuring its starboard side. Notice that the nose wheel turns 90% to lay flat under the pilot's seat when fully retracted. Each main wheel retracts up into its own nacelle.

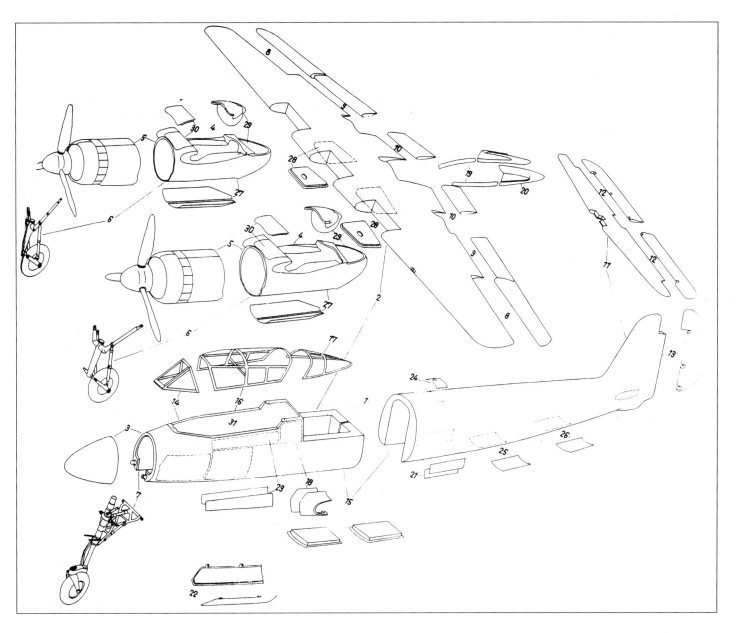

A pen and ink drawing from *WWII* identifying the many component parts of the *Ta 154 A-O*. They include:

01 - Fuselage
02 - Wing
03 - Fuselage hollow plywood nose cap
04 - Engine nacelle
05 - Engine
06 - Undercarriage - main gear
07 - Undercarriage - nose gear
08 - Aileron
09 - Outer wing flap
10 - Inner wing flap
11 - Tailplane
12 - Elevator
13 - Rudder
14 - Cockpit windscreen
15 - Fuel tanks
16 - Forward cockpit canopy
17 - Aft cockpit canopy
18 - Wing fairing
19 - Fairing
20 - Fairing
21 - Wiring cover
22 - Nose wheel closure doors
23 - Cannon trough/ports
24 - Inspection port
25 - Inspection port
26 - Inspection port
27 - Undercarriage doors
28 - Inspection port
29 - Engine nacelle fairing
30 - Engine nacelle fairing
31 - Seats

Courtesy *Military Aircraft #028, Luftwaffe Secret Aircraft 3, 9-1996.*

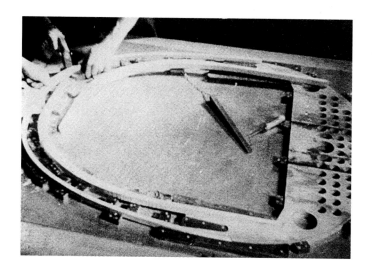

Left: A laminated-plywood canted mounting strut in a jig for assembly. This is where the tail assembly was attached to to the main fuselage. Jigs like this one allowed unskilled worker to make rapid and accurate assembly of *Ta 154's* wooden parts.

The same fuselage, however, with equipment attached. To the right can be seen four air bottles used in the operation of the cannon. To the left and out of sight are two oxygen tanks. Up against the rear bulkhead are what appear to be batteries. In the photo's center bottom is what appears to be the night fighter's master compass.

A fully assembled wooden *Ta 154* rear fuselage aft the cockpit without plywood skin. This component is that section of the fuselage immediately aft the wing. Notice that *Focke-Wulf* was constructing the *154's* wooden fuselage similar to the way a typical metal fuselage with metal stringers but in wood!

A poor quality photo of the *Ta 154 V1* further along in its assembly. Both port and starboard *Jumo 211* engines are complete have been installed to their nacelles. Within the engine cowling nose rings can be seen their radial radiators. If one looks closely in the far right of the photo the starboard side hinged cowling panel on the port engine is open and a technician is bent over addressing some aspect of the *Jumo 211*.

A close-up of the *Ta 154 V1's* nose port side during construction featuring the radial radiators on the port engine and the open cockpit canopy for the radio/radar man.

The *Ta 154 V1* still under construction supported by screw jacks in the background and showing *Kurt Tank* to the left in the photo talking to *Kurt Mehlhorn*, chief test pilot *Hans Sander's* deputy, beneath the cockpit/nose section and appearing to discussing a feature of the fully extended nose gear's oleo strut.

Jewish *KZ* camp workers from the notorious Auschwitz *KZ* in southwest Poland waiting in a well disciplined line to enter their assigned work places on the *Ta 154* laminated plywood component assembly.

The man to the right in this photo is the dreaded *SS Führer Heinrich Himmler*. His *SS* was responsible for providing laborers from *POW* prison camps, slaves, and Jewish men from *KZ* internment camps to manufacture the wood glue produced by *Goldmann Werke* as well as to construct the wooden fuselage, wing, and other components pieces for the series production *Ta 154.*

A poor quality photo of the *Ta 154 V1's* long awaited roll out day at Langenhagen in late June 1943. It's interesting to see large group of men pulling the prototype out of its fitting out hangar.

The new *Ta 154 V1* after its roll out in late June 1943 at Langenhagen. The square opening on the cockpit canopy aft of the windscreen is called the direct vision sliding side window panel.

The camouflaged *Ta 154 V1* with radio call code *TE+FE* up on screw jacks undergoing calibration prior to its first test flight by *Focke-Wulf* test pilot *Hans Sander* on 1 July 1943. It appears that a large number of men have gathered under its starboard wing apparently to view some feature of the starboard main landing gear. Upper surface camouflage was *76 Gray-Green and 75 Gray-Violet*. Undersurface camouflage was *76 Light Blue*. This machine was one of the several *Ta 154s* lost inside its hangar resulting from a bombing raid by *B-17s* belonging to the US 8th Air Force on 5 August 1944.

The *Ta 154 V1* looking so new and shiny. Even the tire on its straight-fork nose wheel leg looks brand new. Notice that this machine has no flame dampers on its *Jumo 211* engine exhausts nor does it appear to have any of its cannon installed. Its radio call code is obscured by the starboard engine/nacelle.

Below: *Kurt Tank* speaking to several of his top engineers after the initial testing their new *Ta 154 V1*. Left to right: *Frau Gotthold Mathias*, unknown man with back to the camera, *Kurt Tank* in coveralls, unknown man, *Gotthold Mathias* in the light colored suit, test flight engineer *Pöhler* wearing sun glasses, and *Flieger-Stabsingenieur Werner Boos*, *RLM* representative assigned to *Focke-Wulf Flugzeugbau*-Langenhagen.

Key *Focke-Wulf Flugzeug* personnel standing out front of their new *Ta 154 V1's* starboard engine at Langenhagen. They include left to right: *Hans Sander* (*Focke-Wulf*), *Professor Schlichting* (Technical High School-Brunswick, *Herbert Wolff* (*Focke-Wulf*), *Dr.-Ing. Heinz Conradis* (*Focke-Wulf*), *Schomerus* (*Messerschmitt AG*), *Husemann* (*RLM* with back to the camera), *Professor A. Betz* (Director of *AVA*-Göttingen), *Professor Blenk* (Director of the Institute of Experimental Aviation), and *Gotthold Mathias* (*Focke-Wulf*).

Gotthold Mathias, Redondo Beach, California. March 1987.
Photo by author.

A tail port side view of the camouflaged new *Ta 154 V1 "TE+FE"* shown outside its hangar at Langenhagen about July 1943.

A starboard side view of the *Ta 154 V1* out on the tarmac at Langenhagen early July 1943 and shortly after its roll out. This brand new prototype has not had its radio call code painted on the aft fuselage. It appears that this machine has no radar array, cannon, or flame suppressors/dampers installed yet.

A nose port side view of the new *Ta 154 V1* with *Kurt Tank* at the controls, engines running, and giving a good view of its initial straight-fork nose oleo strut. This oleo strut was later changed to one which allowed the nose wheel to castor freely. Notice, too, that the aluminum spinner on the twin *VS-11* 3-blade wooden propellers appear to be camouflaged black as well as the propellers. *Kurt Tank* may have test flown the *Ta 154* as many as six times during July 1943.

Focke-Wulf's chief test pilot *Dipl.-Ing. Hans Sander* second from left. He and the others in the photo are at Rechlin Test Flight Center. In the background is a *Fw 189*. *Sander* performed most of the test flying on the *Ta 154* prototypes. Post war *Sander* defended the *154* saying that its controls were as lite as those in a *Fw 190*, a rate of roll about the same as the *Fw 190*, sufficient rudder to climb on one engine...in short a very pleasant machine to fly.

Left: A young-looking *Kurt Tank,* design engineer, at the drawing board at *Focke-Wulf Flugzeugbau,* Bremen.

Kurt Tank, test pilot, at *Focke-Wulf Flugzeugbau. Tank* said that he personally very new design prototype coming out of his factory...he had to otherwise he could only depend on the reviews/comments made by others concerning flying characteristics of each new model. Relying on others wasn't good enough. He had to know for himself.

A poor quality photo of the *Ta 154 V1* in flight as seen from its starboard side. What the stick- like object hanging down into the air stream from beneath the cockpit is likely its nosewheel which has not fully retracted due to hydraulic problems. Prior to landing test pilot *Hans Sander* had to manually put the nose wheel out and lock it.

A poor quality photo of the *Ta 154 V1* in a low level high-speed pass and shown as it passes over a *Fw 190A* parked on the ground. Summer 1943. Langenhagen.

A well publicized and much better image of the same *Ta 154 V1* as shown above. In the lower left hand corner can be seen the one of the propeller blades from the *Fw 190A* on the ground.

The *Ta 154 V1* ending its maiden flight. This flight about occurred two weeks before the promised ten month delivery date *Kurt Tank* and his staff had guaranteed the *RLM* when they began design studies.

Hans Sander is taxiing the *Ta 154 V1* to its hangar area after completing a successful first flight. Notice the numerous well-wishers coming to greet pilot *Sander*.

Hans Sander bringing the *Ta 154 V1* to a stop on the tarmac after the successful first flight. A ground crew man dressed in black is seen directing *Sander* where to bring the prototype to a full stop.

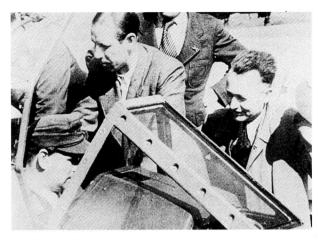

The *Ta 154 V1.* In the cockpit sits a *Luftwaffe* officer from the *RLM.* Behind the windscreen is *Ernst Nipp*, head of the *Ta 154* design team. The man behind the pilot is *Willi Käther*, Technical Director of *Focke-Wulf*.

Kurt Tank is being assisted into the open cockpit of his *Ta 154 V1* "*Moskito*" for his first test flight. Notice how the hinged cockpit canopy opens to starboard.

The *Luftwaffe* officer from the *RLM* is seen deplaning from the *Ta 154 V1. Ernst Nipp* has his left hand on *VS-11* wooden propeller. Behind *Nipp* is *Willi Käther*.

Kurt Tank in the *Ta 154 V1's* cockpit appears to be looking over at his starboard 1,350 take-off horsepower *Jumo 211F* engine.

Kurt Tank dressed in white shirt and necktie is seen here deplaning his *Ta 154 V1*. A good view of the port *Jumo 211F* engine's *VS-11* propeller blade and spinner hub-cover can been seen as well as a portion of its radial radiator.

Kurt Tank is seen coming down the step ladder after deplaning his *Ta 154 V1* at Langenhagen.

Flight Log Of The Focke-Wulf Ta 154 V14						
Flight Number	Date	Take-Off Time	Landing Time	Flight Time In Minutes	Pilot	Co-Pilot
01	25 May 44	13:17	14:00	43.0	Sander	Pöhler
02	27 May 44	8:52	9:01	9.0	Sander	Pöhler
03	27 May 44	11:53	12:08	15.0	Sander	Pöhler
04	27 May 44	14:20	14:30	10.0	Sander	Pöhler
05	27 May 44	14:49	15:03	14.0	Wollank	Pöhler
06	29 May 44	10:35	11:13	38.0	Wollank	Busse
07	29 May 44	15:37	15:54	17.0	Sander	Pöhler
08	29 May 44	16:20	16:45	25.0	John	Wollank
09	30 May 44	16:40	16:54	14.0	Sander	Pöhler
10	30 May 44	17:07	17:22	15.0	Sander	Pöhler
11	30 May 44	17:44	17:55	11.0	Sander	Pöhler
12	30 May 44	18:20	18:30	10.0	Sander	Pöhler
13	30 May 44	18:50	19:08	18.0	Sander	Pöhler
14	30 May 44	19:35	20:05	30.0	Sander	Pöhler
15	31 May 44	10:38	11:55	77.0	Vohl	Pöhler
16	31 May 44	13:40	13:45	05.0	Vohl	Pöhler
17	31 May 44	19:00	19:10	10.0	Vohl	Pöhler
18	01 June 44	08:40	08:46	06.0	Vohl	Pöhler
19	01 June 44	09:36	11:00	84.0	Vohl	Pöhler
20	02 June 44	09:15	09:55	40.0	Sander	Rottke
21	02 June 44	10:40	10:51	11.0	Sander	Rottke
22	02 June 44	11:12	11:36	24.0	Streib	Rottke
23	02 June 44	11:50	12:09	19.0	Galland	Rottke
24	02 June 44	16:58	17:10	12.0	Sander	Rottke
25	02 June 44	19:02	19:19	17.0	Esche	Rottke
26	02 June 44	19:45	20:37	52.0	Sander	Rottke
27	03 June 44	16:48	18:33	105.0	Sander	Rottke
28	03 June 44	19:28	21:10	112.0	Sander	Rottke
29	03 June 44	Na	Na	32.0	Sander	Rottke
30	04 June 44	12:15	12:46	31.0	Malz	Rottke
31	04 June 44	14:15	14:37	22.0	Sander	Rottke
32	04 June 44	14:46	15:04	18.0	Malz	Rottke
33	04 June 44	15:25	15:41	16.0	Malz	Rottke
34	06 June 44	09:55	10:34	39.0	Sander	Rottke
35	07 June 44	18:40	19:00	20.0	Tank	Pöhler
36	07 June 44	19:27	19:55	28.0	Beauvais	Pöhler

The *Ta 154* prototypes were flight tested extensively. For example here is a copy of the flight log for the *Ta 154 V14*. It was flight tested by several of the *Luftwaffe's* great pilots between 25 May 1944 and 7 June 1944. Among its pilots were *Focke-Wulf's* top test pilot *Hans Sander*, *Kurt Tank*, General of Fighters *Adolf Galland*, one of the top test pilots from Rechlin *Heinrich Beauvais*, and famed night-fighter pilot *Oberstleutnant Werner Streib*. Co-pilot on many of *V14's* flights was *Focke-Wulf's* top test flight engineer *Pöhler*. It is not known to this author what became of *Ta 154 V14* at war's end. One historian has suggested that it was used for *Ta 154C* series destruction tests, which means that it was completely consumed in the process.

Top Rechlin test pilots *Otto Berhens* (left) and *Heinrich Beauvais* (right) shown in the cockpit of what appears to be a *Bf 108*. *Otto Berhens* lost his life in Argentina testing *Kurt Tank's* jet-powered *Pulqui II* which had been based on *Hans Multhopp's* war-time *Ta 183*.

Adolf Galland (left), Oberstleutnant Werner Streib, Inspector of Night Fighters (center), Kurt Tank, and Oberst Trautloft, Eastern Inspector on the Staff of the General der Jagdflieger. The long faces all around came after both Galland and Strieb had test flown the Ta 154 V14 at the airfield at Berlin-Staaken on 2 June 1944. Afterward Galland told his long-time good friend Kurt Tank that a fully loaded Ta 154 would be unable to overtake a de Havilland "Mosquito" much less shoot it down. Notice that Galland is not wearing his Ritterkruz around his neck. Göring had accused his Luftwaffe pilots of cowardice for failing to stop the Allied bombing of the Reich. Göring claimed that those pilots who had won the Ritterkruz really didn't deserve it because their victories had been inflated. So Galland took his off and refused to wear it...sort of a mutinous statement one would think.

Dipl.-Ing. Hans Sander, chief test pilot at Focke-Wulf Flugzeugbau and the major test pilot on the Ta 154. He was among the best in Germany and is shown here in the cockpit of a Fw 190A.

A close up view through a Fw 190A's port side cockpit windscreen of Hans Sander.

Hans Sander deplaning from his *Fw 190A*.

Left: *Focke-Wulf Flugzeugbau's* chief flight test engineer *Pöhler* (left) wearing sunglasses and *Kurt Tank* (center).

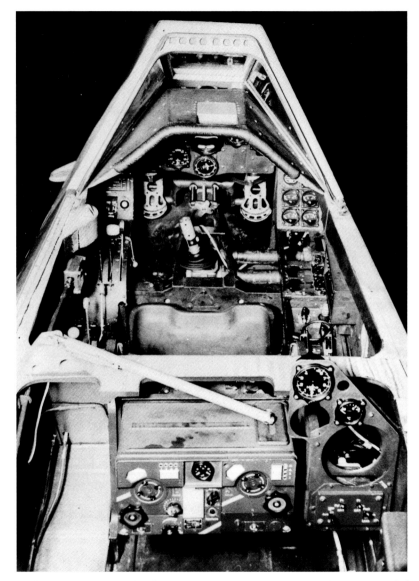

A view into the cockpit of the *Ta 154 V1* looking forward from the radio/radar operator's seat. A full view of the pilot's instrument panel is obscured because of the camera angle. The light colored square aft the armored windscreen is where its *Revi 16B* reflector gun sight would be later installed. It appears that the pilot's armored head rest has not yet been installed, either.

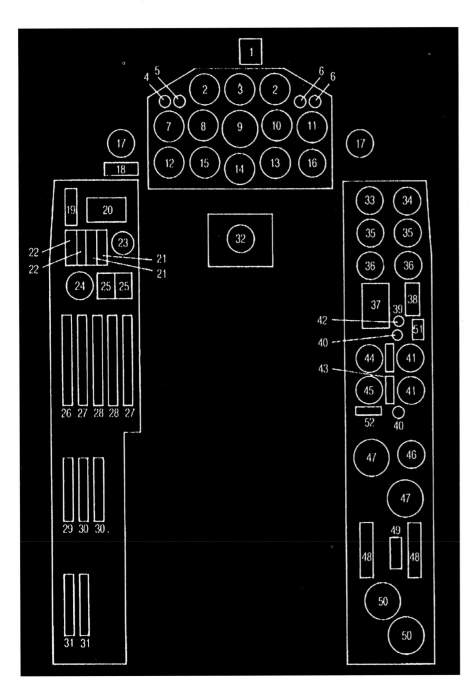

A pen and ink drawing of the *Ta 154 V1's* instrument panel. The *Ta 154's* instrument panel under when several changes/modifications. For the *V1*, at least, this diagram includes:

01 - *Revi 16B* reflecting gunsight
02 - RPM indicator
03 - Double manifold pressure gauge
04 - Radar indicator
05 - Pilot heat indicator
06 - Engine pump indicator
07 - Side radar
08 - Air speed indicator
09 - Artificial horizon
10 - Variometer
11 - Magnetic compass
12 - Height radar
13 - Radar altimeter
14 - Slaved gyrocompass
15 - Sensitive altimeter
16 - Automatic direction finder
17 - Fuel/oil pressure
18 - Landing gear switch
19 - Three position flap
20 - Gear and flap indicator
21 - Propeller feather control
22 - Electric fuel pumps
23 - Emergency electrical system control
24 - Dual hydraulic pressure gauge
25 - Magneto switches
26 - Throttle friction lock

27 - Propeller pitch controls
28 - Throttles
29 - Fuel tank selector
30 - Fuel mixture controls
31 - Turbos (*V1* and *V2*)
32 - Clock
33 - Oxygen indicator
34 - Oxygen pressure
35 - Oil temperature
36 - Coolant temperature
37 - Ammunition counter
38 - Warm air control
39 - Cabin heat indicator
40 - Fuel supply warning light
41 - Fuel gauges
42 - Autopilot master switch
43 - Autopilot emergency disengage
44 - Gyro instrument switch
45 - Radar master switch
46 - Oxygen flow valve
47 - Hydraulic system valves
48 - Starter switches
49 - Fuel injection switch
50 - Cowl flaps
51 - Cabin heat control
52 - Windshield defog control

A pen and ink drawing illustrating the location of the major *Ta 154 V1* cockpit instruments and placed in the cockpit panel.

Seen in this photo is an incomplete *Ta 154 V1's* instrument panel. Rudder pedals, control stick, for example, are in place, however, the instrument panel has yet to be installed although two small diameter metal tubing are there waiting to be connected to instrument(s).

The is the cockpit of the *Ta 154's* radio/radar operator. It appears fairly complete at the time the photo was taken although the *FuG 212A* radar scope/aiming apparatus remains to be installed on top of the square box-like radar operator's panel. The open hole to the right is probably where the slaved gyro compass would have been located. Notice that the cockpit fuselage walls have been constructed out of wood.

The *FuG 212A Lichtenstein* cathode radar screen as it probably would have appeared inside the *Ta 154 A-4* two seat night fighter. The screens left to right include: distance/range, vertical deflection, and horizontal deflection. This apparatus would have been covered by a flexible rubber boot for the radio/radar operator to peer into.

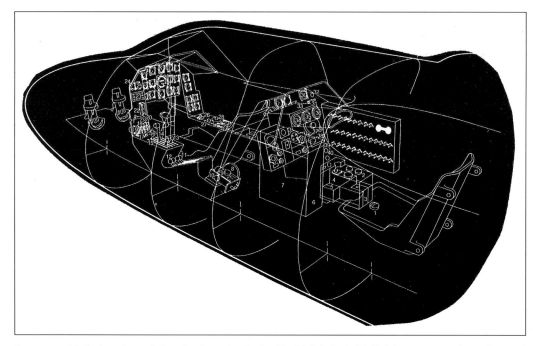

A pen and ink drawing of the dual cockpit of a *Ta 154 A-4* night fighter as seen from its port side. Although the identification numbers are hard to read they include:

01 - Emergency flap extension valve	21 - Landing gear switch
02 - Radar receiver	22 - Flap selector buttons
03 - Radio junction box	23 - Landing gear and flap indicator panel
04 - *FuB1* 2F ILS receiver	24 - Radar operator indicator
05 - Loop antenna	25 - Radar selector switch
06 - Hydraulic hand pump	26 - Ammunition supply indicator
07 - *FuG 220 Lichtenstein* transmitter/receiver	27 - Gyro master control
08 - Elevator trim	28 - Light rheostat
09 - Aileron trim	29 - Fuel quantity gauge
10 - Rudder trim	30 - Nonsensitive altimeter
11 - Fuel cut off and tank selector	31 - Radar equipment
12 - Superchargers	32 - Heating system indicator
13 - Propeller setting levers	33 - *Lichtenstein* search apparatus
14 - Throttles	34 - Range scope
15 - Friction lock	35 - Vertical deflection scope
16 - Hydraulic system button	36 - Horizontal deflection scope
17 - Ignition switch	37 - Slaved gyro compass
18 - Mixture controls	38 - Radar operator's panel
19 - Mechanical landing gear position indicator	39 - *FuG 16 ZE* navigation/communication
20 - Emergency electrical system	40 - Homing receiver
	Courtesy *Monogram Close-Up 22 Moskito*.

This off-setting panel labeled "*V 232*" on the starboard side of a *Ta 154 A-4* two seat night fighter appears to be the *FuG 16 ZE* navigation/communication panel.

Shown in the top center of this photo is the radio/radar operator's rear cockpit canopy in the up/open position on *Ta 154 A-4* two seat night fighter under construction at Langenhagen.

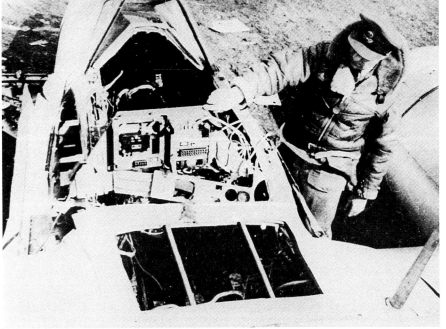

Above Left: The rear metal seat for the radio/radar operator in a *Ta 154 A-4* two seat night fighter. It appears that armor head rest would be just forward of the one piece wing main spar and the run-way for various wires, cables, and tubing attached to it.

Left: Shown in this photo is the remains of probably a *Ta 154 A-4* two seat night fighter's cockpit. An American officer is standing next to its starboard side with his right hand pointing to a heavily damaged radio/radar operators instrument panel. Whether the damage was deliberate or other is not known to this author. At war's end a lot of *Luftwaffe* aircraft were deliberately blown up by their crews.

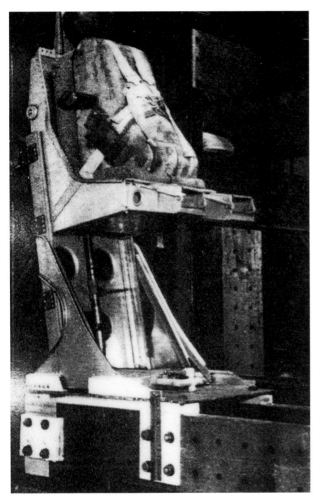

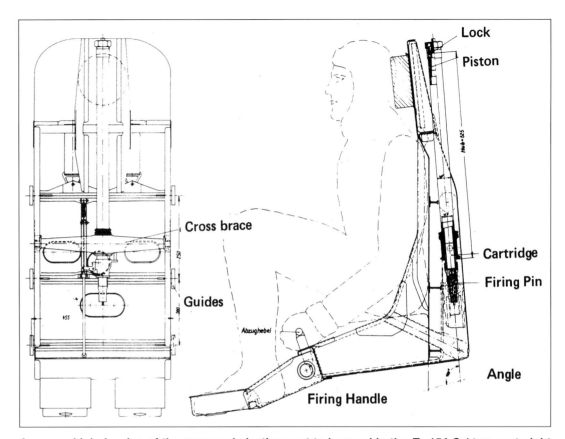

A pen and ink drawing of the proposed ejection seat to be used in the *Ta 154 C-1* two seat night fighter and also the *Ta 254 A-1* two seat night fighter.

What appears to be a mockup of the proposed ejection seat to be used in the *Ta 154 C-1* two seat night fighter and the *Ta 254 A-1* two seat night fighter. Or perhaps it is the real item undergoing pre-installation testing. This author does not know for sure.

The proposed method of ejecting the pilot and radio/radar operator from a *Ta 154 C-1* and *Ta 254 A-1* two seat night fighters. It appears that *Focke-Wulf* designers were working on an arrangement where the two men would be ejected through an open panel on the underside of the cockpit.

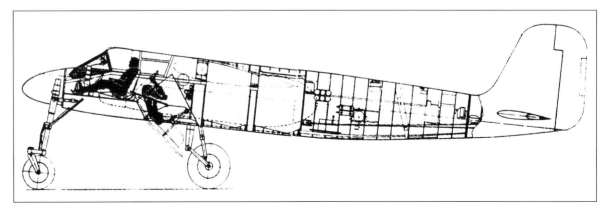

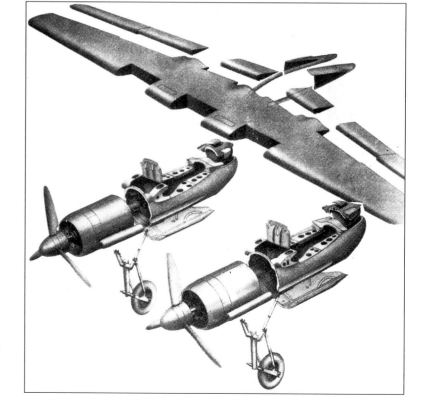

The test-firing of a prototype pilot's ejection seat reportedly built by the German flight-suit manufacturer *Dräger. Heinkel AG* was also experimenting with their own ejection seat designed by *Dip.-Ing. Karl Butter.* The need for an ejection seat came about as *Luftwaffe* interceptors, night fighters, and fighter aircraft were expected to go to higher and higher altitudes to attack high-flying Allied bombers. Then, the *RLM* had the ever-present fear that America would introduce their *Boeing B-29s* over Germany. It never was but still *Luftwaffe* pilots had to be equipped should they need to bail out at high altitudes.

Focke-Wulf engineers didn't have a very big selection of in-line liquid cooled piston engines to choose from in early 1943 when they were designing their wooden *Ta 154* two seat night-fighter prototype. They had to settle for the *JunkersMotorenWerke* (*Jumo*) *211F,* an inverted *V12,* and producing only 1,340 horsepower at takeoff. *Kurt Tank* wanted the *V12 Jumo 213E* which provided 1,776 horsepower at takeoff but it wasn't available by the end of September 1943 as *Jumo* had promised. Each *Jumo 211F,* covered by its metal cowling, was attached to the wing's leading edge via a metal alloy forged cantilever support bar within an all wooden nacelle which in turn was attached to the wing as shown in this pen and ink drawing.

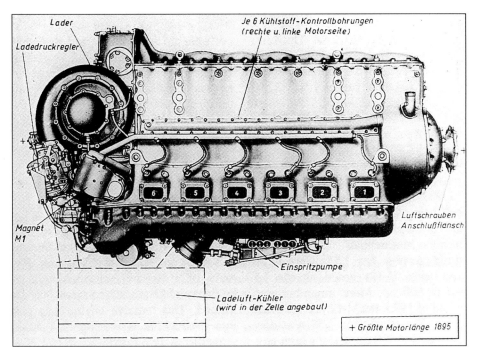

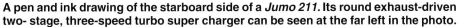

Labels on drawing:
- Lader
- Ladedruckregler
- Je 6 Kühlstoff-Kontrollbohrungen (rechte u. linke Motorseite)
- Magnet M1
- Einspritzpumpe
- Luftschrauben Anschlußflansch
- Ladeluft-Kühler (wird in der Zelle angebaut)
- + Größte Motorlänge 1895

A pen and ink drawing of the starboard side of a *Jumo 211*. Its round exhaust-driven two- stage, three-speed turbo super charger can be seen at the far left in the photo.

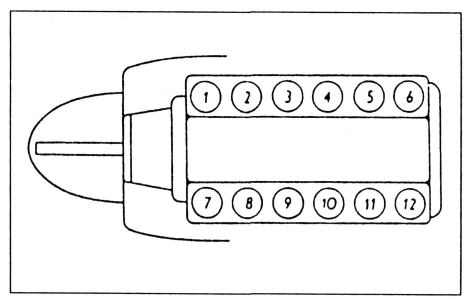

Above Right: The *Jumo 211* and *213* had twelve cylinders configured in a "V" arrangement. This pen and ink drawing shows how they were numbered from 1 to 12 as seen from looking up at the engine from the ground.

Right: A photo of a inverted *V12 Jumo 211* as seen from its nose port side of the type which powered the *Ta 154 V1* two seat night fighter prototype. The square openings near the bottom of the engine(rocker-arm covers) are the exhaust ports. Above the exhaust port are small diameter metal tubing are fuel lines feeding the fuel injectors.

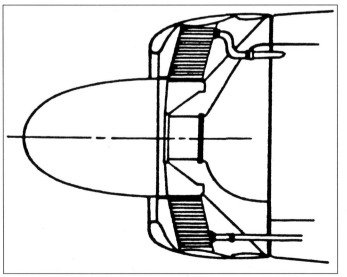

The same port *Jumo 211* on the *Ta 154 V1* but with its *VS-9* 3-bladed wooden propeller mounted. The metal spinner covering the propeller hub will be installed next.

Above Left: The port *Jumo 211* on the *Ta 154 V1* seen here without its *VS-9* 3-bladed wooden propeller and giving a good view of the engine's radial radiator which was mounted around the engine's reduction gear.

Left: A pen and ink drawing of the *Jumo 213A* from a side view showing the location of its radial radiator to the propeller hub and reduction gear casing on the engine.

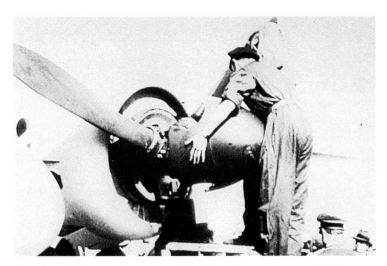

The size of the aluminum propeller hub spinner was huge! Although light weight, an engine technician has his arms full with the spinner as he positions its over the propeller hub.

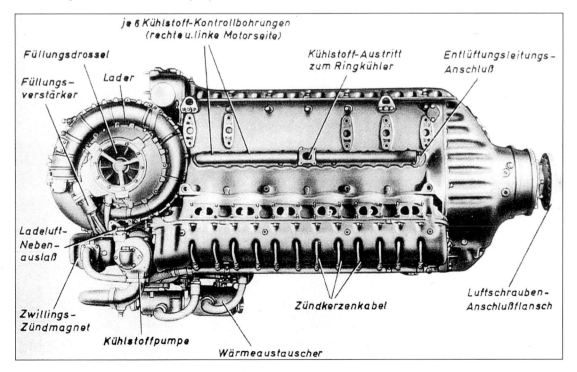

je 6 Kühlstoff-Kontrollbohrungen
(rechte u. linke Motorseite)

Füllungsdrossel

Füllungs-
verstärker

Lader

Kühlstoff-Austritt
zum Ringkühler

Entlüftungsleitungs-
Anschluß

Ladeluft-
Neben-
auslaß

Zwillings-
Zündmagnet

Kühlstoffpumpe

Wärmeaustauscher

Zündkerzenkabel

Luftschrauben-
Anschlußflansch

The port side of the *Ta 154 V1* two seat night fighter with its propeller hub spinner attached and complete for flight testing. No exhaust flame suppressors are installed on this machine. However, as a night fighter the *Ta 154 A-4* would have been equipped with exhaust flame suppressors to minimize RAF gunners from being able to identify the aircraft in the night sky due to its bright red exhaust.

A pen and ink drawing of the starboard side of the *Jumo 213A-1,* 12 cylinder inverted Vee. The large round object to the far left in the drawing is the engine's exhaust-driven two-stage, three-speed turbo supercharger.

A *Jumo 213A-1* showing its starboard side and its forged metal cantilever mounting bearer of the type that would be used to power the *Ta 154 C & D* versions as well as the *Ta 254A* version . The *Jumo 213A* was a *12* cylinder inverted V, liquid-cooled turbo super charged aero-engine producing 1,776 horsepower (take off). The entire engine was attached by only four bolts to the *Ta 154's* wooden fire-proof bulkhead. Notice that the air intake to the supercharger is covered over by a cloth rag.

A close up view of a *Jumo 213A's* starboard side cantilever mounting bar. To the right of the photo is the upper cantilever bar and beneath it is its supporting tube. Both items were through bolted to the fire wall by a single bolt as was the cantilever mounting bar on the opposite side of the engine.

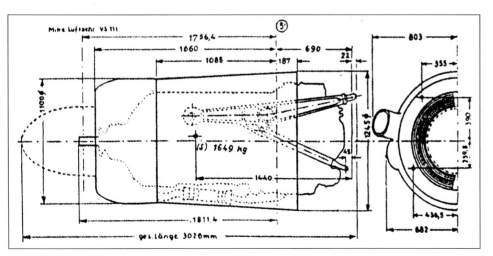

A pen and ink drawing showing the outline of the *Jumo 213A* inside its engine nacelle on a *Ta 154C/D* version, supported by its cantilever forged alloy mounting bearer bar, and attached to the *Ta 154's* fire-proof engine mounting bulkhead.

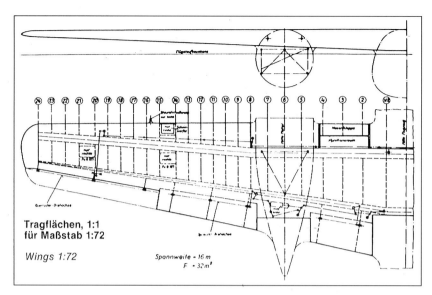

Tragflächen, 1:1
für Maßstab 1:72

Wings 1:72

Spannweite = 16 m
F = 32 m²

A pen and ink drawing outlining the port side wing of a *Ta 154* and the approximate location of its port engine mounting to the fire-proof bulkhead.

A photo of a actual *Jumo 213A* of the type to have been installed in the series production *Ta 154 C-1* two seat night fighter. The engine in this photograph appears to be complete with all of its accessory equipment and so on required for a flight ready power plant.

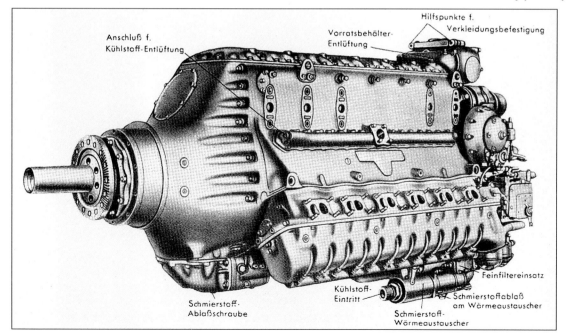

Anschluß f. Kühlstoff-Entlüftung

Vorratsbehälter-Entlüftung

Hilfspunkte f. Verkleidungsbefestigung

Feinfiltereinsatz

Schmierstoff-Ablaßschraube

Kühlstoff-Eintritt

Schmierstoff-Wärmeaustauscher

Schmierstoffablaß am Wärmeaustauscher

A pen and ink drawing of a *Jumo 213A* engine of the type used in the *Ta 154 C-1* two seat night fighter as viewed from its front propeller shaft port side. The *Ta 254 A-1* two seat night fighter was also scheduled to be powered by this engine.

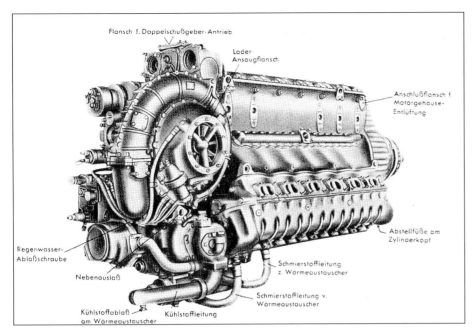

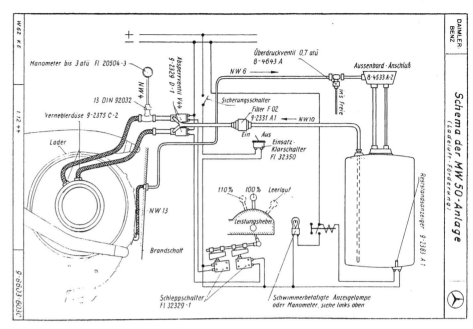

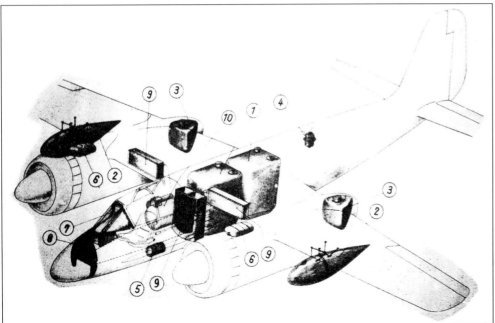

The *Jumo 213A* frequently was equipped with the *MW50* power boost system. The *MW50* was a methanol-water injection system. This pen and ink drawing shows the layout of a *MW50* system installed on a *Jumo 213* engine. The tank holding the *MW50* liquid is at the far right in the drawing. Through a variety of valves, controls, tubes, the *MW50* enters into the *213's* supercharger as shown in the far left.

Above Left: A pen and ink drawing of a *Jumo 213A* as seen from its rear starboard side. It's round exhaust- driven super charger and pumps almost occupy the entire rear portion of this engine.

Left: A pen and ink drawing of the fuel and oil storage containers required for operation of the *Jumo 213A* in a *Ta 154 C-1* two seat night fighter. These tanks include:

01 - Fuel tanks - internal	06 - Coolant tank
02 - Fuel drop tanks	07 - Armored windshield screen
03 - Oil tanks	08 - Armor plating
04 - Pump, electric	09 - Ammunition boxes for cannon
05 - Hydraulic oil tank	10 - *GM-1* engine power boost system tank

Courtesy *Ta 154*, *R.T. Murray*, ISO Publications, London, 1979.

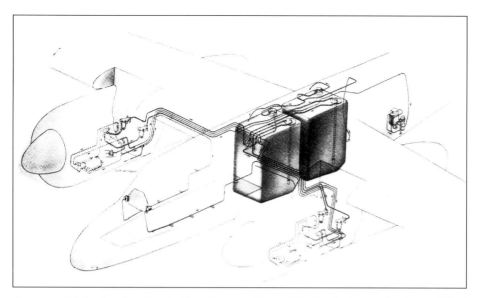

A pen and ink drawing illustrating the location of the fuel storage tanks and fuel lines installed in the *Ta 154 A-4* two seat night fighter. Courtesy *Ta 154, R.T. Murray*, ISO Publications, London, 1979.

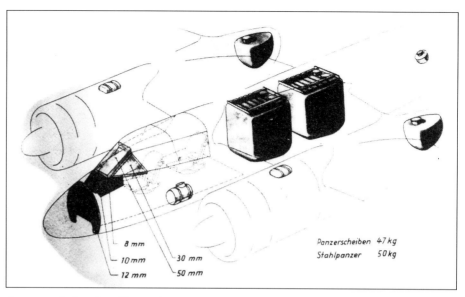

A pen and drawing illustrating the armor plating surrounding the fuel tanks, oil tanks, and cockpit on a *Ta 154 A-4* two seat night fighter. Courtesy *Ta 154, R.T. Murray,* ISO Publications, London, 1979.

The *Ta 154 V7* with radio call code "*TE+FK.*" This machine has had a engine exhaust flame suppressor installed as seen here on its port, port side engine. Flame suppressors or dampers were required equipment for a night fighter to help them avoid detection by RAF heavy bomber gunners and "*Mosquitos.*" Flame suppressors used by the *Luftwaffe* looked like large, black metal, round tubes or pipes.

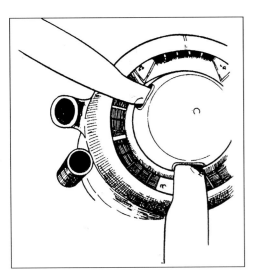

A pen and ink drawing of an exhaust flame suppressor/damper on the starboard side of a port engine of a *Ta 154 A-4*. Courtesy *Military Aircraft #028, Luftwaffe Secret Weapons #3, 9-1996.*

A typical engine exhaust flame suppressor/damper on a *Luftwaffe* night fighter and similar to the style used on the *Ta 154 A-4* two seat night fighter. Notice that the exhaust stacks come out from the engine and merely go into the flame suppressor and with air coming into the suppressor at the open front, exhaust gases flow out the open end.

In the lower left-hand corner of this photo can be seen the long black tube which was an exhaust flame suppressor/damper on the port side of *Ta 154 A-4's* two seat night fighter's starboard engine.

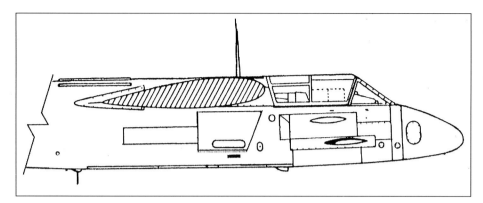

A pen and ink drawing of the starboard side of a *Ta 154 A-4* two seat night fighter and featuring its starboard cannon muzzle blast troughs/ports. The square-like box aft the cannon trough/ports and directly beneath the leading edge of the wing was where *Luftwaffe* armorer's gained access to the two cannon.

The starboard side of a *Ta 154 A-4* two seat night fighter and showing its twin cannon muzzle blast troughs/ports. The upper port accommodated a *1xMG 151* 20 mm cannon. The lower port was for a *1xMK 108* 30mm cannon. There were similar cannon troughs on the opposite side of the fuselage.

A *Ta 154 A-4* two seat night fighter showing its long pipe-like exhaust flame suppressors in place. Digital image by *Mario Merino*.

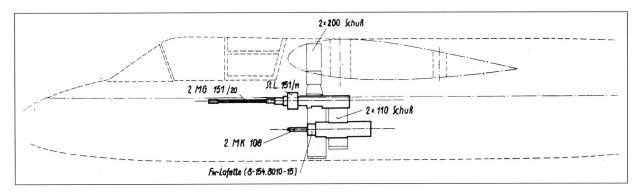

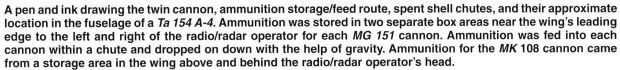

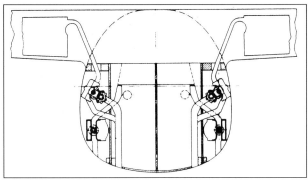

A pen and ink drawing the twin cannon, ammunition storage/feed route, spent shell chutes, and their approximate location in the fuselage of a *Ta 154 A-4.* Ammunition was stored in two separate box areas near the wing's leading edge to the left and right of the radio/radar operator for each *MG 151* cannon. Ammunition was fed into each cannon within a chute and dropped on down with the help of gravity. Ammunition for the *MK* 108 cannon came from a storage area in the wing above and behind the radio/radar operator's head.

A pen and ink cross-sectional drawing showing the placement of the *Ta 154 A-4's* two seat night fighter four cannon and the ammunition belt delivery path from their storage in the wing. In the fuselage are shown *2xMG 151* cannon (top) with 200 rounds per cannon and *2xMK 108* cannon (bottom) with 110 rounds per cannon.

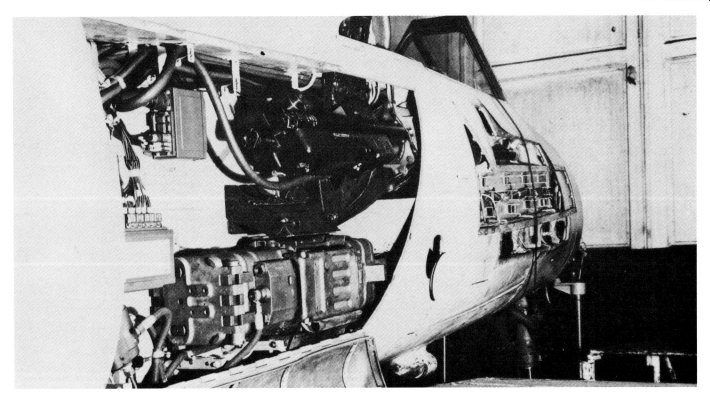

The port side of the *Ta 154 V1* under construction and showing its open port side weapons bay. The lower cannon is a *MK 108* 30 mm cannon with 110 rounds. The upper cannon was the *MG 151* 20 mm with 200 rounds.

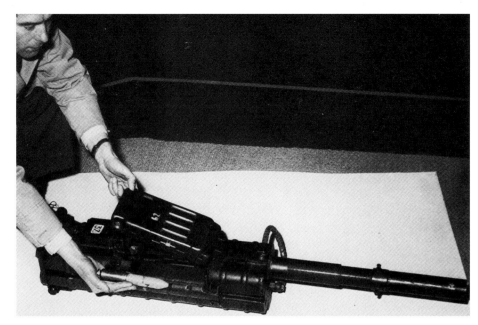

The size of a *MK 108* 30mm cannon is huge as seen in this photo. Noted aviation historian *Alfred Price* is seen in the left of the photo and in his right hand is a typical 30 mm cannon shell with its explosive head.

The *Ta 154 V4* with its modified, raised aft cockpit rear canopy proposed for the two seat day- fighter version *Ta 154 A-4*.

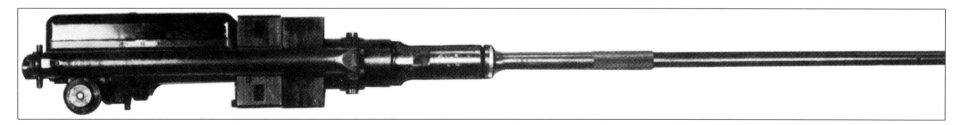

A typical *MG 151* 20 mm long barrel cannon of the type to be installed in the fuselage of the series production *Ta 154 A-4* two seat night fighter.

Left: Shown in this photo is the port side raised rear canopy on the *Ta 154 A-1* two seat day fighter where the rear gunner sat back to back to the pilot but higher as shown in this photo so he could operate a twin barrel *MG 81* 7.92 mm cannon. The shells the *MG 81* this cannon fired were the same as those used in the *Mauser* (1938) infantry rifle.

A *MG 81* 7.92 mm twin barrel cannon of the type to be installed in the two seat day-fighter version of the *Ta 154 A-1*. This double cannon was capable of a rate of fire in excess of 3,200 rounds per minute (1,600 rounds per cannon).

Above Left, Opposite Page: An *MG 81* 7.92 mm cannon installed in the rear cockpit of a *Luftwaffe* fighter. This installation would have been similar to what was planned for the two seat day fighter version known as the *Ta 154 A-1* and here it is shown with its twin barrels extending out well past the aft cockpit canopy.

A pen and ink drawing of the *MG 81* 7.9 mm cannon featuring a side and top view. Muzzle velocity was feet per second 2,315 feet per second [705 meters per second].

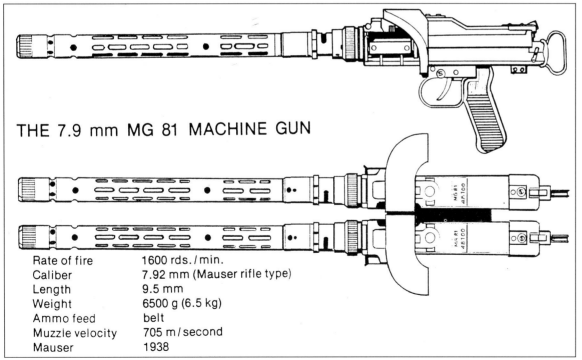

THE 7.9 mm MG 81 MACHINE GUN

Rate of fire	1600 rds./min.
Caliber	7.92 mm (Mauser rifle type)
Length	9.5 mm
Weight	6500 g (6.5 kg)
Ammo feed	belt
Muzzle velocity	705 m/second
Mauser	1938

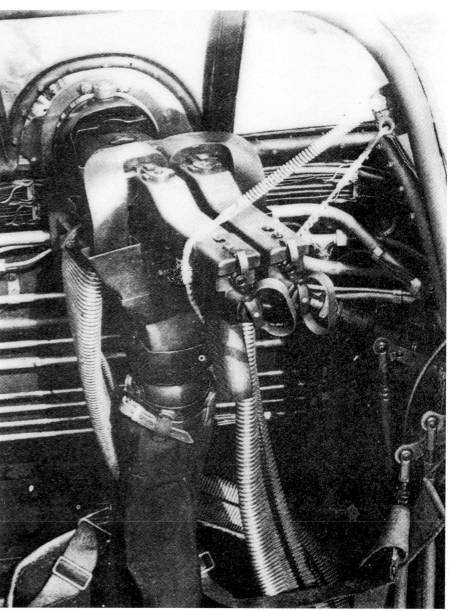

A defensive weapon considered for use in the *Ta 154 A-2* single seat day fighter version by its *Focke-Wulf* designers was a single *MG 131* 13 mm cannon mounted in an electrically-operated dorsal turret, an example of which is shown in this photo of a *Do 217E-2* as it is being refueled.

This is how the double barreled *MG 81* 9.72 mm cannon might have appeared to the pilot has he turned his head around to speak with the rear gunner on the *Ta 154 A-1* two seat day fighter version.

An overhead view of the *MG 81*. Both guns have ammunition belts attached (loaded) and the gunner is pulling the cock-handle of the starboard *MG 81* to load the first round into the chamber. Both guns were fired by pressing a single trigger, usually located on the port gun.

This is how the gunner in the two seat day fighter version of the *Ta 154 A-1* might have looked as he was preparing to fire the flying machine's twin barrel *MG 81* 9.72 mm cannon.

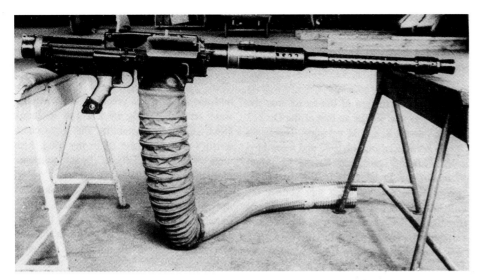

The *MG 131* 13 mm cannon on a pair of sawhorses. The fabric tube hanging down is the chute tube for exhausting spent 13 mm shell casings.

A dorsal electrically operated turret containing a single *MG 131* 13 mm cannon with 500 rounds of the type considered for installation in the single seat day fighter version known as the *Ta 154 A-2.*

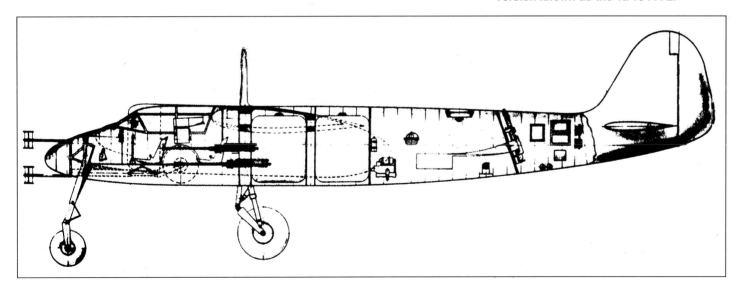

Another type of offensive armament considered is shown in this pen and ink drawing of the initial design concept of the *Ta 154* prototype. On its nose is the aerial array for the early *FuG 212* "mattress bedspring" radar. This night fighter is also being proposed with a "*Schräge Musik*" 2x*MG 151* 20 mm cannon and it is being shown pointing forward at an 70% oblique angle from the horizontal.

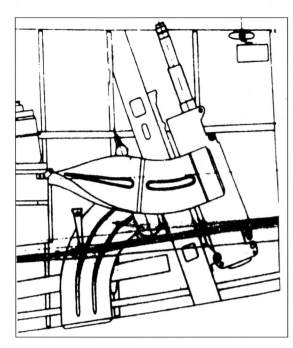

A pen and ink close-up drawing of the proposed "*Schräge Musik*" 2x*MG 151* 20 mm cannon installed in the aft fuselage of a *Ta 154* and seen with its barrel(s) pointed up and obliquely.

A *Junkers Ju 88* with a pair of "*Schräge Musik*" *MG 151* 20 mm cannon one of which, at least, was proposed for installation in the new *Ta 154.*

The *Ta 154C* and the *Ta 254 A-1* were projected to carry additional offensive cannon from those to be used in the *Ta 154 A-1*. In the *Focke-Wulf* drawing the upper illustration appears to have *3xMK 108s* plus *2xMG 151* "*Schräge Musik*" in the fuselage aft the wing's trailing edge. In the lower illustration this version appears to have *2xMK 108s* plus *1xMG 103* all mounted in the fuselage below the cockpit. In addition this version appears to have *2xMG 131s* in the aft fuselage firing to the rear.

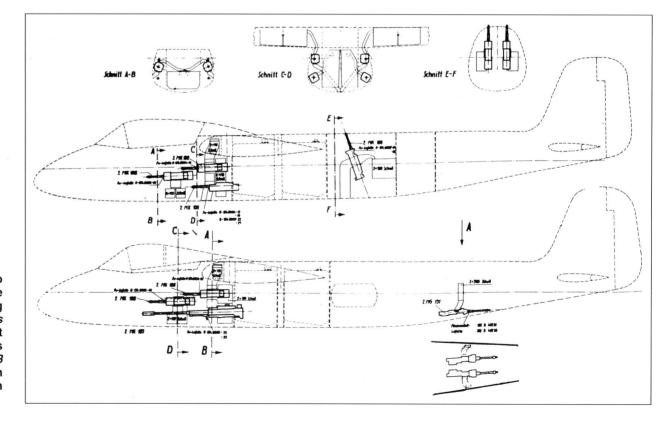

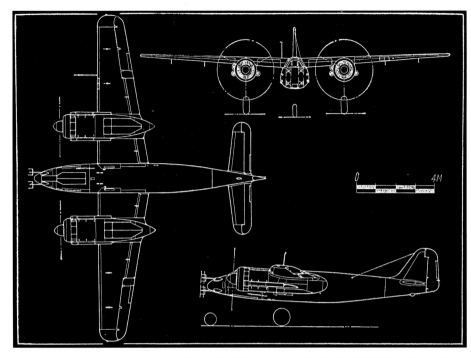

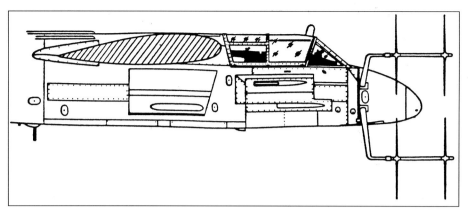

A pen and ink drawing of the *Ta 154* featuring a starboard side view of its *FuG 220's* SN-2 aerial array. Courtesy *Karo-As Models*.

A pen and ink 3-view drawing of the *Ta 154* shown with its *FuG 212* "mattress bed-spring" radar aerial array.

A photo of the *Ta 154 V3* "*TE+FG*" and carrying a radar aerial "mattress bed-spring" array for a *Telefunken FuG 212 Lichtenstein C-1* radar system with its 4-pole antenna. The *V3* was lost inside its hangar at Langenhagen due to a bombing raid on 5 August 1944.

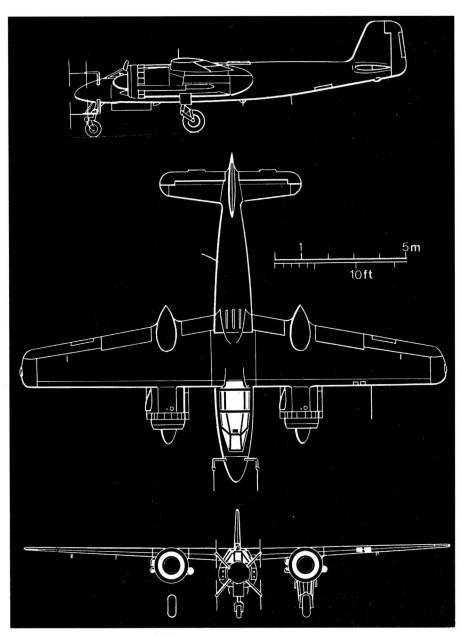

A nose starboard side view of the *Ta 154 V-15* with its *FuG 220* "*Hirschgeweih*" nose- mounted antenna array for its *Lichtenstein SN-2* radar set.

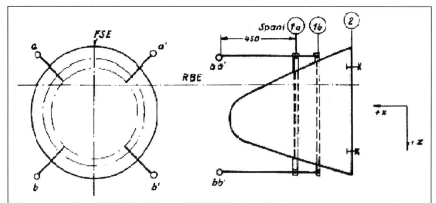

Pen and ink 3-view drawings featuring the *Ta 154 A-O/U2* (*V-14*) and its so-called "*Hirschgeweih*" antenna array for its *FuG 220 Lichtenstein SN-2* radar.

A pen and ink drawing of the showing the exact locations of its four *FuG 220* external radar support arms entered and attached to the *Ta 154's* wooden nose cone.

A close up view of one of the four *FuG 220* external radar support arms as it leaves the *Ta 154's* wooden nose cone.

The detached under side of the wooden nose cone for a *Ta 154*. Notice that the support arms for the four *FuG 220* external radar can be seen.

A close-up view of the *FuG 220 Lichtenstein* search apparatus as mounted in the *Ta 154 A-4* two seat night fighter.

Another view of the *Ta 154 A-4's FuG 220 Lichtenstein* search apparatus and the opening for its slaved compass (left) and the "*V-232*" *Lichtenstein* selector panel (right). The triple cathode screen container apparently would be mounted on top of the search apparatus box shown.

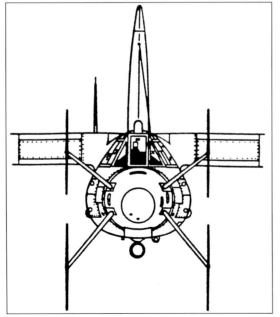

A close-up view of the *Ta 154's* "*V-232*" *Lichtenstein FuG 220* selector panel.

A pen and ink drawing featuring a *Ta 154 A-4's FuG 220's SN-2* aerial antenna radar array nose on. Courtesy *Karo-As Models*.

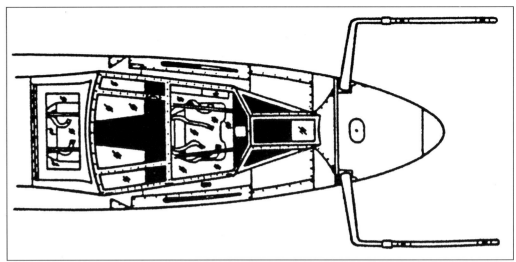

A pen and ink drawing of a *SN-2* aerial antenna array on a *Ta 154A-4* two seat night fighter as it would appear when looking down from above. Courtesy *Karo-As Models.*

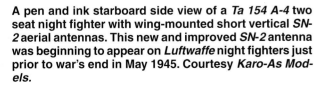

The nose of a *Ta 154 A-4* two seat night fighter featuring its *FuG 220 SN-2* aerial antenna radar array.

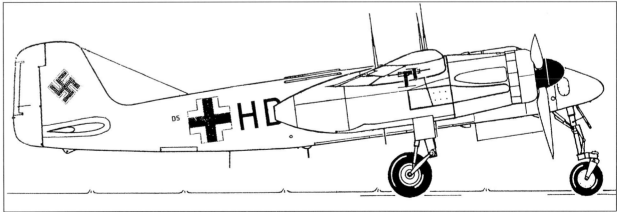

A pen and ink starboard side view of a *Ta 154 A-4* two seat night fighter with wing-mounted short vertical *SN-2* aerial antennas. This new and improved *SN-2* antenna was beginning to appear on *Luftwaffe* night fighters just prior to war's end in May 1945. Courtesy *Karo-As Models.*

A nose port side view of a *Ta 154 A-4* two-seat night fighter with wing-mounted *FuG 218 SN- 2* aerial antenna and camouflaged in a single dark color.

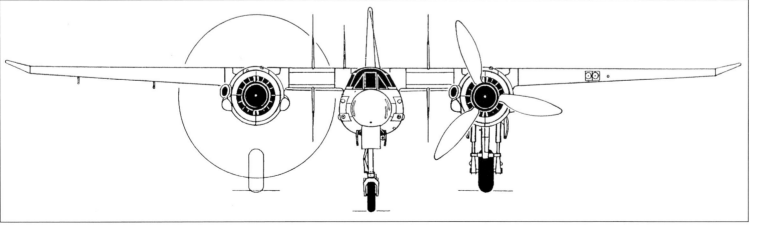

A pen and ink drawing featuring the nose on view of a *Ta 154 A-4* two seat night fighter with its wing-mounted *FuG 218 SN-2* aerial antenna. Notice, too the up-turned (dihedral) wing tips. This feature first appeared on later production versions and was intended to improve lateral stability. Courtesy *Karo-As Models.*

The light camouflaged *Ta 154 A-4 D5+HD* down in a field on 30 April 1945 and featuring a *SN-2 Lichtenstein* wing-mounted aerial antenna. The *Jumo 213A* powered *Ta 154 A-4* featured *VS-9* wooden propellers and the machine was assigned to *3./NJG3*. Notice how the wooden propeller has broken off close to the propeller hub which was typical for this type of material when an aircraft bellied in.

An overhead view of the *Ta 154 A-4 D5+HD* from its starboard wing side. Two of its several dorsal *SN*-2 antennas can be seen at the far left of the photo. Two more are barely visible at the wing's leading edge center wing just aft the radio/radar operator's seat.

The *Ta 154 V-1* prototype up on screw jacks showing off its tricycle-style landing gear fully extended.

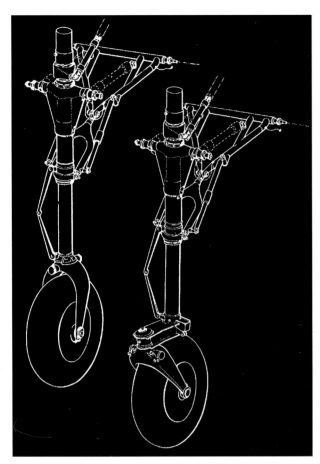

Two styles of nose gear appeared on the *Ta 154.* The simple oleo strut (left) appeared on the *V1* prototype. Later the nose gear was modified to a full castoring nose wheel (right) beginning with the *V4* and all *Ta 154s* appeared with this feature thereafter.

The diameter of the *Ta 154 V1's* nose wheel can be gauged by this photo. The nose wheel reaches up to *Focke-Wulf's Dip.-Ing. Herbert Wolff's* knee.

A prototype nose oleo strut and wheel intended for the *Ta 154 V1* undergoing testing at *Focke- Wulf Flugzeugbau* in early 1943. In this photo it appears that the oleo strut is being tested for its hydraulic damping and is pretty much depressed down as it goes through repeated simulated weighted landings.

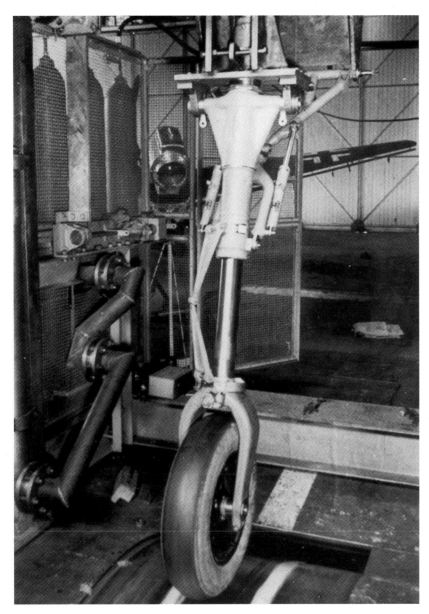

The prototype nose wheel oleo strut for the *Ta 154 V1* (the non castoring version) its hydraulic cylinder appearing fully extended as weight is being eliminated as it would be when the wheel leaves the runway and prior to retraction into the fuselage.

The complete nose wheel assembly mounted in the new *Ta 154 V1* under construction and minus its fuselage nose cone.

The *Ta 154 V4* shown upside down on runway at Tamewitz due to a failure of its new castoring nose wheel as it was making its take off run.

Above Left: A full castoring nose wheel as mounted in *Ta 154 V4.* The *V4* was modified to a two seat day- fighter version carry a rear-firing *MG 81* cannon. The *V4* crashed during take-off on 1 June 1944 at Tamewitz believed to be due to a malfunctioning of its new castoring nose wheel.

A good view of the *Ta 154's* (*V4*) open three piece nose wheel gear closure doors.

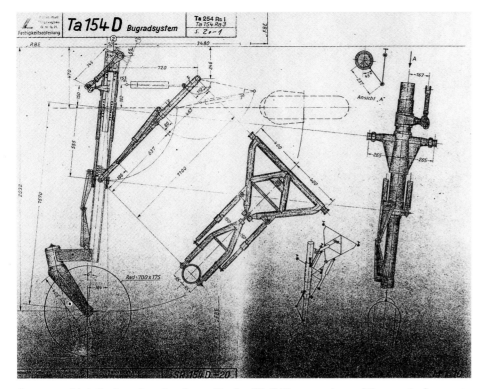

A pen and ink drawing of main landing gear on the *Ta 154* featuring the port main wheel, oleo strut, and gear attachment structure. Courtesy *Ta 154, R.T. Murray,* ISO Publications, London, 1979.

A pen and ink 3-view drawing from *Focke-Wulf Flugzeugbau* of the castoring nose wheel on the *Ta 154 V4* and all other later machines.

The main wheel landing assembly seen installed on *Ta 154 V1 TE+FE*'s port side. The *TE+FE* is being supported by screw jacks.

A main wheel assembly for the series production *Ta 154* showing its tire, main support, and aft hydraulic oleo strut.

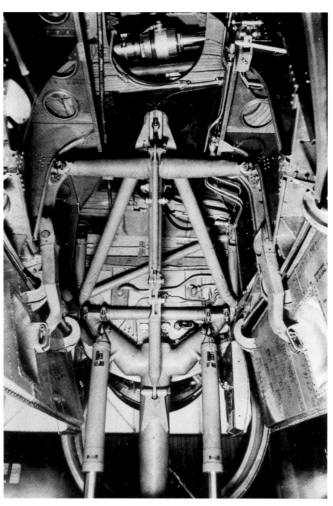

A view inside the *Ta 154 V1's* main wheel nacelle showing the main wheel gear attachment and refraction mechanism.

A close-up view of the upper portion of the main wheel gear and its attachment points inside the wooden nacelle.

The camouflage pattern applied to the *Ta 154 V3 TE+FG* shown with a solid color on its vertical stabilizer as well as the dorsal area of its fuselage. The *TE+FG* has an early nose-mounted *FuG 212 Lichtenstein* radar array.

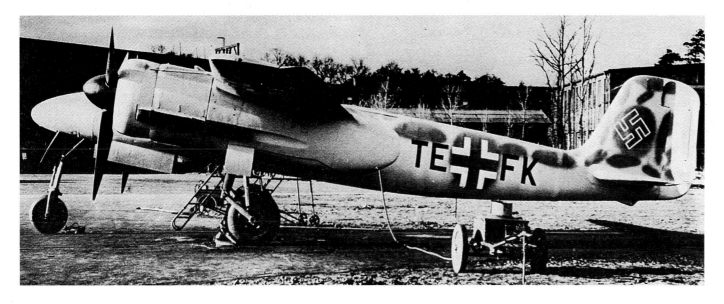

The camouflage patten applied to the *Ta 154 V7 TE+FK* with its two tone dapple pattern as seen on its tail assembly and upper fuselage surface. This machine was lost along with several other *154's* during a USAAF bombing raid on Langenhagen 5 August 1944.

The camouflage pattern applied to the *Ta 154 A-0 TQ+XE* with a solid color on its vertical stabilizer and a small mount of molting on its aft fuselage.

The camouflage pattern applied to a *Ta 154 A-1/R1* two seat day fighter found abandoned at Lechfeld war's end.

The same Lechfeld-found *Ta 154* machine at war's end as above but viewed closer to its starboard side tail assembly.

The camouflage pattern applied to the *Ta 154 V1* prototype and shown after its roll out on in July 1943. No armament or radar array have been yet installed.

The *Ta 154 V1* after its radio call code *TE+FE* had been applied. A small amount of camouflaging had been applied, too.

The two-tone dapple camouflage pattern applied to the *Ta 154 V7 TE+FK*'s upper surfaces. This prototype was destroyed during the USAAF's 5 August 1944 bombing of *Focke-Wulf's* Langenhagen facilities.

The camouflage pattern appearing on the *Ta 154 A-4 D5+HD*'s severed tail assembly's upper surfaces appears to be a solid light color. The camouflage appearing on the upper surface of the port horizontal stabilizer seems to be a two-tone dapple similar that which appeared on the *Ta 154 V7 TE+FK*.

One of the several *Ta 154's* destroyed at Langenhagen on 5 August 1944 due to a bombing raid. Its radio call code begins with *"TQ+—"* so therefore it is not entirely certain which *154* this might be although its fuselage appears to be longer than other *154* prototypes. For this reason, the machine shown in this photo may be the *V22* with the lengthened fuselage.

This is how *Focke-Wulf*-Langenhagen looked after its facilities, assembly halls, and air field was systematically destroyed by USAAF bombers on 5 August 1944. It was pretty much unuseable for its previous activities for the remaining months of the war.

A *Ta 154 V3* or later its camouflage appearing as a solid light stain.

The port nose side of an unidentified *Ta 154* with an open cockpit is seen in the far left of this photo featuring a stack of five new-looking *Jumo 004Bs* at war's end reportedly discovered at Lechfeld.

The flipped over *Ta 154 A-4 D5+HD* shown in this photo does not give very many clues to its camouflage pattern especially since its entire tail assembly was severed off. What appears of its port side fuselage and engine nacelle is of a solid light color.

This severely damaged *Ta 154 V8,* which appears to have bellied in, does not give any clues to its camouflage pattern although the starboard engine nacelle (left) appears to be a solid light color. This machine was the first *154* to be powered by twin *Jumo 213A* engines when it was destroyed on 6 May 1944.

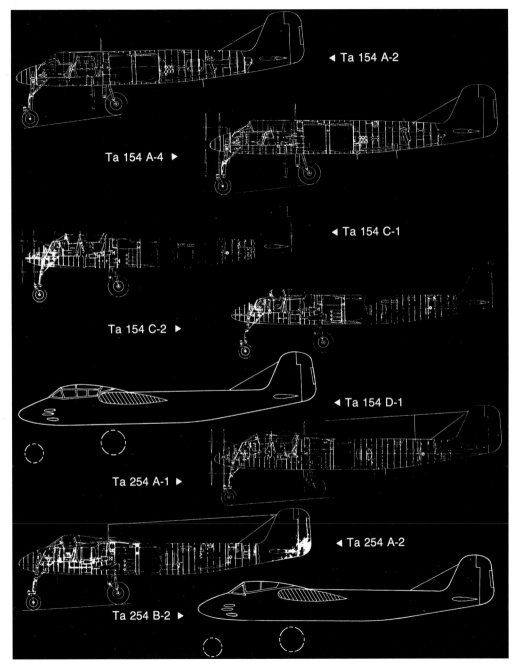

◀ Ta 154 A-2

Ta 154 A-4 ▶

◀ Ta 154 C-1

Ta 154 C-2 ▶

◀ Ta 154 D-1

Ta 254 A-1 ▶

◀ Ta 254 A-2

Ta 254 B-2 ▶

A pen and ink drawing featuring the starboard side of several *Ta 154* and *Ta 254* versions. From top to bottom they include:
01 - *Ta 154 A-2* – *Jumo 211N* powered single-seat day fighter with 2x66 gallon drop tanks; 02 - *Ta 154 A-4* – series built two-seat night fighter (actual number built unknown) with *FuG 212* and *220* radar aerial arrays; 03 - *Ta 154 C-1* – *Jumo 211N* powered two-seat night fighter, metal nose, lengthened fuselage, and ejection seats; 04 - *Ta 154 C-2* – *Jumo 213A* powered single-seat day fighter/bomber with a sliding cockpit canopy, metal nose, and *GM-1* injection boost system; 05 - *Ta 154 D-1* – *Jumo 213E* powered two-seat night fighter prototype for the *Ta 254 A-1*; 06 - *Ta 254 A-1* – *Jumo 213E* powered two-seat night fighter with metal nose cone and ejection seats; 07 - *Ta 254 A-2* – two-seat day fighter with a sliding cockpit canopy and *VS-19* 4-bladed propellers; and 08 - *Ta 254 B-2* – *Daimler-Benz 603L* powered two-seat day fighter

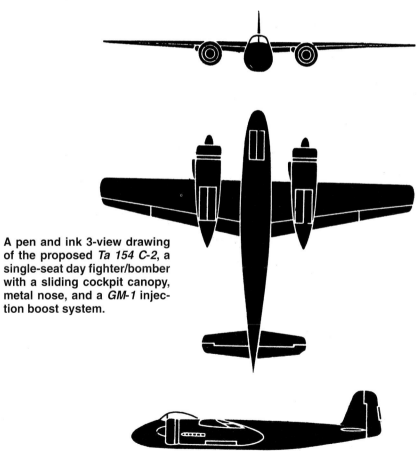

A pen and ink 3-view drawing of the proposed *Ta 154 C-2*, a single-seat day fighter/bomber with a sliding cockpit canopy, metal nose, and a *GM-1* injection boost system.

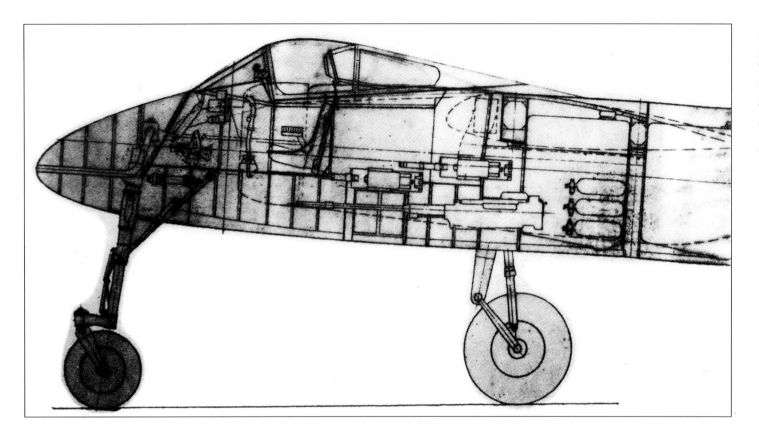

A proposed advanced production version shown in this pen and ink drawing is known as the *Ta 154 C-2*. This would have been a single seat day fighter/bomber with a blown bubble-type sliding cockpit canopy. The idea *C-2* was dropped in favor of the so-called *C-3* which was to have been a two seat reconnaissance machine.

A pen and ink drawing of the port side of the proposed *Ta 154 C-1* single-seat day fighter/bomber and featuring its bubble cockpit canopy and metal nose cone. In addition, this version would have had a longer fuselage than the series production *Ta 154 A-4*...5,425 mm [17.79 feet] for the *C-1* versus 4,675 mm [15.34 feet] for the *A-4*.

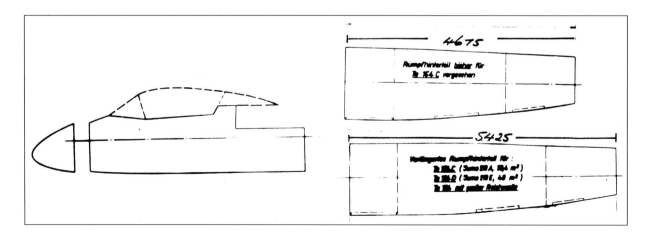

Proposed changes to the *Ta 154 A-4* and known as the *Ta 154 C* further evolved into what *Focke-Wulf* was calling the *Ta 254.* Basically the *Ta 254* was a high-altitude multi-purpose machine with a 30% increase in gross wing area over the basic *Ta 154 A-4.* Two engine types were proposed for the *Ta 254* machines: the *Jumo 213A-1* would power the so-called *Ta 254A* while the *Daimler-Benz DB 603L* would power the *Ta 254B.* A four-bladed *VS-19* propelled would have been used with the *Jumo 213* while the *DB 603L* would have turned *VDM* propellers.

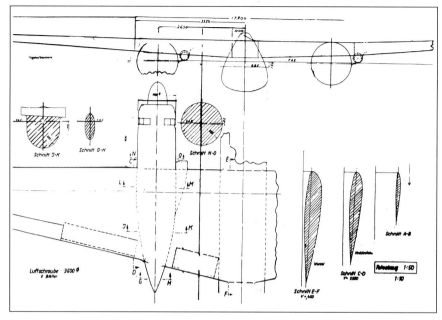

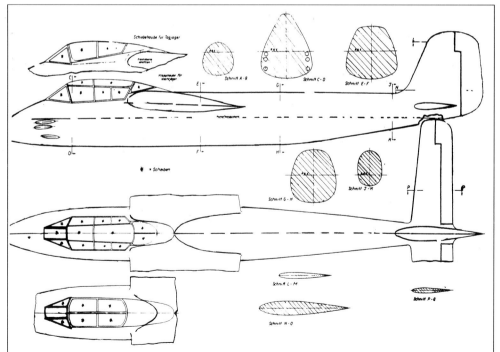

The proposed *Ta 154 C-3* two seat reconnaissance powered by twin *Jumo 213 A-1* engines. Initially the *C-3's* were to be reconnaissance machines but by Spring 1944 this version was dropped in favor of a two seat day fighter version stilled called the *C-3.*

A pen and ink drawing by *Focke-Wulf* featuring the port side of three *Ta 154 A-4s* as a *Sprengstoffträger* or bomber. It was intended that these special bombing machines would loaded with high explosives as shown in the drawings and than piloted to the target. When approaching the target the pilot would bail out saving himself. In one version of the *Sprengstoffträger* the cockpit would have been moved aft allowing for more explosives but equally important to allow the pilot a safe exit out of the machine. In its final version, six *Sprengstoffträger's* are known to have been built, the pilot and copilot strapped in their seats were to have been ejected down out of the *Moskito* if necessary. Nothing is known regarding their final disposition at war's end.

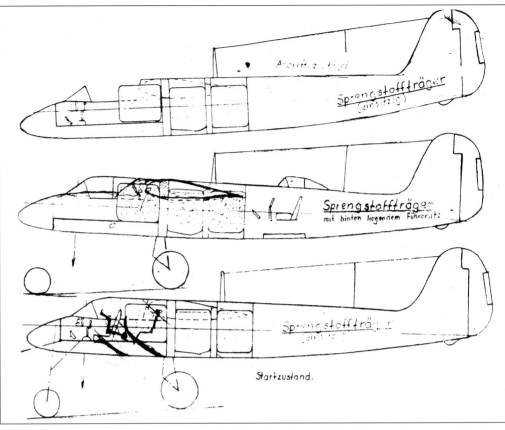

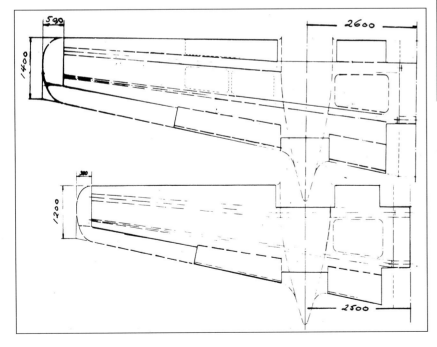

A pen and ink drawing by *Focke-Wulf* showing how the 30% increase in gross wing area would be obtained in the *Ta 254* version.

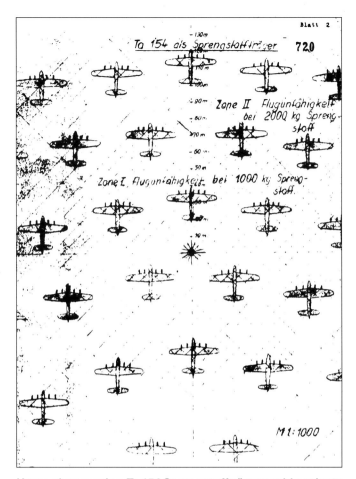

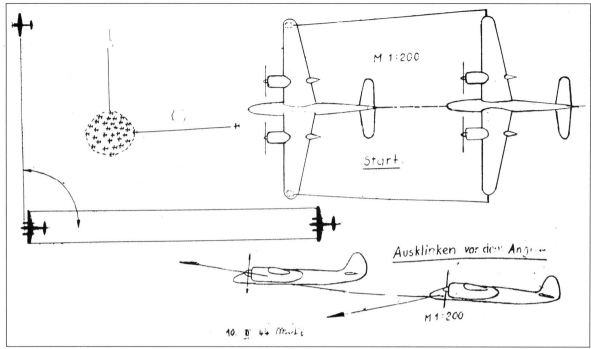

Another planned use of the *Ta 154* at war's end was to load it with high explosives and then tow it with another *Ta 154* up to the attitude of a *B-17* bomber pack and aim it head on so that it would enter into the bomber pack. As the two *Ta 154* approached the bomber pack the towing *Ta 154* would unhook itself and allow the explosive-filled *Moskito* to go right in the mist of the *B-17s*. At this moment the explosive-filled *Ta 154* would be detonated. *DFS* had been experimenting with one aircraft towing another for this very purpose. As far as this author is aware no such towing attempts were made using the *Ta 154 Moskito*.

How a slow-moving *Ta 154 Sprengstoffträger* could navigate in and around all the fighter escorts and yet be able to reach deep inside the bomber pack without being shot out of the sky by escorting *P.47 Thunderbolt's* or *P.51 Mustangs* is unknown? But here is the concept. In the center of the pen and ink drawing (from *Luftwaffe* records) of the Allied bomber pack is a "***" and this is the location where the pilots flying the high explosive-laden *Ta 154* wanted it to reach before it was detonated and its pilots already having bailed out. It is doubtful that the slow moving *154's* would ever come close to the bomber pack be intercepted long before reaching the bomber pack and destroyed.

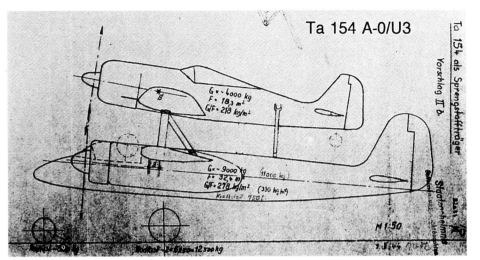

Ta 154 A-0/U3

The *Ta 154* as the explosives-laden bottom portion of the *Mistel* combination. This was the idea of taking an unwanted bomber loading it with high explosives and place a pilot in a *Fw 190* or *Bf 109* and place it on the back of the bomber and fly the combination to a target with the fighter detaching itself once it had aimed the bomber at its target. This idea of *Mistel* was to send these explosive-packed bombers to Moscow and destroy the numerous electric generating facilities located there and which served a great portion of the USSR's armaments industry. This was known as *Operation Eisenhammer*. Several *Mistel* flights are known to have taken place but none deep into the USSR although as many as 80 *Mistel* combinations were built usually with *Ju 88* as the explosive-laden aircraft. No *Ta 154's* are known to this author to have been outfitted for use in the *Mistel* program, however, German reports claim that approximately eight *Ta 154* were to have been turned into 8,400 pound bomb.

A close-up of a *Mistel* combination: a *Fw 190A* upper and a *Ju 88* lower. The largest bomb carried by a German heavy bomber such as the *He 177* was 5,500 pounds. With the *Mistel* the lower aircraft could be loaded with 8,400 pounds of high explosives and aimed right into a target.

Also from the publisher

Messerschmitt P.1101

An Illustrated Series on Germany's Experimental Aircraft of World War II

David Myhra

X PLANES OF THE THIRD REICH SERIES
An Illustrated Series on Germany's Experimental Aircraft of World War II
Messerschmitt P.1101
David Myhra

Powered by a single HeS 001A turbojet engine, Woldemer Voigt, who had artfully crafted the Me 262, ran out of time before he could make the 1101's design "jell" as he struggled to produce the world's first variable wing sweep, ultra light weight interceptor, and armed with Germany's state-of-the art wing-mounted air-to-air guided missiles. Post-war, Bell Aircraft sought to carry on Voigt's planning and resolved to make the complicated mathematics of light weight, variable wing sweep and wing-mounted weapons come together in a single aircraft design. The result was the Bell X-5, and it too, was disappointing. This photographic history of the Me P.1101 by David Myhra features mostly previously unpublished photos, three-view line drawings, and stunningly realistic photos of a 1101 scale model.

Size: 11" x 8 1/2"   ■   over 100 b/w photographs and line drawings   ■   64 pp.   ■   soft cover   ■   ISBN: 0-7643-0908-0 $9.95

X PLANES OF THE THIRD REICH SERIES
An Illustrated Series on Germany's Experimental Aircraft of World War II
Heinkel He 162
David Myhra

Over 200 images, including three-view drawings, comprise this one of a kind photo album on the He 162. Included are photos of the He 162 in wartime service with JG 1, and the later surrender of at least thirty-one flight ready He 162s to British ground forces at Lech on 8 May 1945. Subsequent test flights of He 162s in post-war England, USSR, South Wales, Australia, and the United States are also covered. No other aviation publication has ever assembled this large a quantity of images of the He 162 in a single volume.

Size: 11" x 8 1/2"   ■   over 200 b/w photographs and line drawings   ■   96 pp.   ■   soft cover

ISBN: 0-7643-0955-2 $14.95